The Naked Truth

The Gospel According to Singles

By
E. Marcel Jones

Acknowledgements

—◊—

To my God for your promises, reconciliation, and unconditional love; Christ Jesus for your forgiveness, salvation, and life; Holy Spirit for your gifts and continual presence in my life

To my wife for being a constant supporter of my ideas and goals; for praying me through some crazy times; and to my son for my daily hug bugs and for reminding me about the innocence of love

To my mom, dad, sister, and brother for investing in me, believing in me, sacrificing your last, and for nurturing a passion for reading and writing early in life

To my pastor and friend, Gary L. Faulkner – For mentoring me and raising the standard in ministry; you are truly a role model

To my church family, Cummings Street Baptist Church and the Singles Crew - For allowing my ministry to take root and for being patient with my growth spurts

To other local and nationally recognized Christian Ministries – For allowing me to share with you through the years – Mt. Ararat Baptist Church (Trezevant, TN); Mt. Pisgah Baptist Church (Memphis); New Direction Christian Church (Memphis); Soul Winners Baptist (Memphis); Temple of Praise C.O.G.I.C. (Memphis); Union Baptist Church (Dallas, TX)

To my Copyeditor – Ms. Betty Sims…thank you for your golden eagle eyes. Your correction pen is mighty, my sister!

To my mentors and professors for helping me develop my gift…Dr. Martin, you helped lay the foundation

To the 5,6,7 Connection…God is still using us

To my buddies Daryl, Errol, Everett, and Pechone – For holding me accountable and pushing me to finish what God had begun

To Kingdom Quality Communications for assisting with the set up of <u>The Naked Truth Singles Conference 2009</u> – … Renee Malone and the crew, you guys are awesome!

Table of Contents

—ɯ—

Introduction

—ͻͻͻ—

This single scripture provides the backdrop for this entire project—The Naked Truth.

I Timothy 4:12 – *"Don't let anyone look down on you because you are young (SINGLE), but set an example for believers in speech, in life, in love, in faith, and in purity."*

Reflecting on the lives of those who were young and single in the scriptures, I realize that far too many singles today are living defeated lives. I hear their constant cries of being despised by their congregations, society, and even their own family members. In the scriptures, Paul, Joseph, and even Jesus Christ faced similar obstacles, yet they remained victorious in their daily living and service toward God.

Throughout my single years, the stories of those singles in the scriptures were the catalyst of encouragement that molded my life. Through their experiences and perseverance, I understood the scriptures better and clearer. I learned of divine placement through Joseph's story. His character taught me the necessity of living a life of integrity despite what others around me were doing or the direction they were taking. Through the life, death, and resurrection of

Christ, I recognized the value and weight of sacrifice and the purposeful service of the work of the ministry.

Because I was profoundly helped by those who led by example in the Word of God, I wanted to offer this same hope to singles all over the world. One cannot deny that these are perilous times, even more so for the Christian singles that are attempting to live according to God's Word. For this reason, my strongest desire became to provide singles with sound spiritual truths by which to live and on which to hold. Consequently, this project, <u>The Naked Truth</u>, was inspired by this strong desire and from my own life experiences. In fact, in keeping with the title, I actually had to become NAKED to write each chapter. I had to strip myself of my past mistakes and wrong turns. I had to remove layers of mistrust and doubt in my own God given abilities. I had to become exposed and in turn expose my life before you the reader in order for people to be blessed.

Having been single for thirty-eight years, I know first-hand how trying the life of a Christian single can be. As you follow my journey in these pages, you will catch glimpses of my testimony — unclothed and stripped to the bare truth. You will see how as an eighteen year old, I embraced my singleness as freedom — freedom to date, freedom to stay out late, and freedom to make my own choices. When I turned twenty-five, I recalled viewing my single years as periods of growth. I grew spiritually, physically, and emotionally. And, boy did I experience the growing pains! By age twenty-eight, it was obvious that I was no longer the person I was in my teens. By my mid-thirties, a new single had emerged. God had performed a spiritual makeover. Thank God I did not resemble what I had been through. Like a rose bush surrounded by fertilizer and manure, I used the decay to my advantage and grew from the experience. The fragrance I was releasing was a sweet smelling savor until God's nostrils.

The E. Marcel that once took life for granted was finally living responsibly. There was actually the resemblance of a mature man. However, I had a rude awakening. There was something missing in my life — A helpmate! At first, I struggled with the idea that maybe God was calling me to a life of celibacy. Maybe this was as good it was going to get for me. The more I wrestled with this notion, the more intense the feeling became that there was someone out in this huge world waiting on me to complete her. Strange, huh?

Well, God did send me a helpmate. He could not have chosen a better partner for me. We *complete* each other. She is what I need to be competent, and I am everything that her soul has ever longed for in a man! Well, okay, maybe that is a bit of a stretch, but I am what she needs from a mate to be totally equipped for God's service.

As you read my Christian experiences, keep in mind that I have been where you are and have walked some of the same roads. No, I have not been in YOUR shoes, but as you read, you will discover that I have traveled similar paths. Does this make me authorized to write to singles? Yes, indeed! You bet your Aunt Beatrice's peach pie it does! Think about this; who is really authorized to write to singles? Would it be someone who is still single and is ambivalent about marriage and commitment? Or would it be someone who has been married for many years and is out of touch with singles today? In my assessment, it is really not about the marital status of the author but about the passion in the author's heart. He must be passionate about singles! Writing to singles is about allowing the breath of the Holy Spirit to rest upon every single word penned in each chapter. Once God's signature is on the document, it is official!

Now, understand something else about this project. The contents of this book left my hands a while back. It was as if God lifted the lines off each page, pulled each chapter together in the order he wanted them, poured his voice into the pages, rewrote the beginning and ending, and then handed it back to me to have published. What an awesome God!

Along the way, of course, there have been many disappointments and road blocks that have attempted to keep me from publishing The Naked Truth. But, God had it in his hands each time. And, when I was ready to receive the idea of publishing again, he entrusted it back into my hands. There is a Word waiting for you in the contents of this book. The Word is that there is no time like the present to serve God!

If you read the Bible closely, you will find that many of the most influential Biblical characters were used by God at the peak of their singleness. Yet, in an era when the harvest for saved souls is ripe, the laborers are few. There are singles that have become paralyzed by their past or incapacitated by the bureaucracy of church leadership. On one hand, many choose to remain inactive in their service to the Lord because of what wrongs they committed in the past; they refuse to accept God's complete forgiveness and cleansing. Still others encounter those reluctant church leaders and congregations that are against singles serving in various leadership positions or in select ministries. Nevertheless, there is no excuse for NOT serving God! There is no more convenient time than the present to give God your all. There will never be another moment like right now to allow God complete access to the gifts and talents he has blessed you with so far.

I travel quite a bit because of my job. One of the things I love to do while driving is listen to various radio stations. One particular morning while driving, I tuned in to a station that carried the National Public Radio (NPR) program that is considered to be a scholarly station. I love the news reports and on-air journals the program shares. One particular morning, the program was dedicated to a photographer who had died after a long career of capturing some of the world's key events and people.

One of his photos featured a blind boy with no arms sitting with his face buried in a book. Upon first glimpse of the photo, the boy appeared to be sound asleep. However, the caption below the photograph revealed that this young blind boy without arms was actually reading the Braille embossed book with the tip of his nose. The sad thing is that hundreds of young people in the United States who are blessed with arms, eyes, and the ability to read choose to remain illiterate. No excuse! Likewise, some of us have the capacity to do great things for God yet choose to remain inactive in our kingdom work.

My prayer for you as you read the contents of this book is multifaceted. I pray you discover God's anointing and favor for your life. I pray that your lifestyle lines up with God's purpose and that you intentionally increase your quite time alone with Him. As you read, I encourage you to do the following: Record your emotions and reactions in the margins of the pages; scribble scriptures that support various points made throughout the book. If the book blesses you, purchase one for a friend and another one for a special teen-ager in your life. Also, please know that this book is not meant to be read in one sitting. Like a crock pot, you must slowly allow the flavor of each chapter to marinate your soul's craving to know God more intimately and enjoy the feast set before you.

Section 1

In the Beginning God…

Two Times One
By E. Marcel Jones

Two people entwined together
Temporary?
Or, will it last forever

A knot that holds and grips
Around the waists
Between the lips

It's you; It's me
Passionate
Yet, so free

Chapter 1

Take a "God" Look At Yourself

—ɷ—

Psalms 139:14 - *I praise you because I am fearfully and wonderfully made; your works are wonderful, I know that full well.*

Take a *GOD* look at yourself and tell me what you see. No, it is not a typo; I asked you to take a God look at yourself for a reason.

To take a good look at yourself is to become critical of the imperfections and gloat over the seemingly perfections of your body, personality, possessions, and achievements. However, to take a God look at yourself is to realize the awesome woman or man of God you have been created to become. As you take a God look at yourself, the bad news is that God is not through with you yet. However, the good news is ALSO that God is not through with you yet. You are a work in progress. To look at your life now does not even touch the surface of what he is molding you to become. In fact, your future at this point is not predicated solely on where you are right now. Notice, I said it is not based "solely" on where your lot is today. In other words, neither today nor yesterday have the last say so about who you are to become in God's kingdom.

If you suffer from a low self image, it may be the result of some emotional abuse encountered in the past. Or, maybe your esteem issues are due to the physical structure or characteristics of your body. Regardless to the cause, it is vital that it be repaired quickly. If left unchecked, low esteem can lead to bigger issues such as drug use or abuse and/or sexual promiscuity. Drug use and sexual acts have often been used in an attempt to mask the real problem. Because there is much work for you to do, you cannot remain in a low state. God has a mission personally for you, and it has your full name on it. For that reason, suit up and stop looking at yourself so critically. Instead, begin to take a God look at yourself. In other words, allow the Word of God to reflect who you are and how He views you. Hold the Bible up and reflect on the following verses of scripture:

> *Genesis 1:26, 31* – Then God said, "Let us make man in our image, in our likeness, and let them rule over the fish of the sea and the birds of the air, over the livestock, over all the earth, and over all the creatures that move along the ground. God saw all that he had made, and it was very good…

> *2 Corinthians 3:4-5* – Such confidence as this is ours through Christ before God. Not that we are competent in ourselves to claim anything for ourselves, but our competence comes from God.

As you take a God look at yourself, your life begins to take on a new outlook. Things, persons, and situations do not look the same when you understand what God has designed you to become. You find that you are not as critical of others and their shortcomings when you know that God has the final word in your life's successes. If truth be told, you become so in tuned into ensuring your reflection is glaring the glory of

God that you do not even waste time criticizing others who are not where you are. H. Jackson Brown declared, "Let the refining and improving of your own life keep you so busy that you have little time to criticize others."

> *John 15:4* urges us to imitate or become like Christ. "Abide in Me, and I in you. As the branch cannot bear fruit of itself, unless it abides in the vine, neither can you, unless you abide in Me." (NKJV).

To abide in Christ is to clone Him. To clone Christ is to be like Him in such a way that you literally take on his characteristics. The more Christ-like characteristics you embody, the more your inner man is strengthened. To clone Christ essentially means:

a. To know Him
b. To be as Him
c. To take on His character
d. To imitate Him

Note: *You cannot imitate Christ without taking on his nature. You cannot take on his nature unless you truly know Him. So spiritually, when we clone Christ, we inherit the character traits from Christ. In essence, we inherit our spiritual looks from our heavenly father.*

Genetically speaking, we are the product of borrowed genes from both our mother and father; what we borrow, essentially, becomes who we are. The results of some of these genes show up on the outside. There are some genetic dispositions, however, that remain undetected until a test is conducted.

Spiritually speaking, there are traits that remain dormant in us as well. Much like our physical genes, these traits can also remain hidden until tested. For example, when Jesus was tempted by the enemy, the character of Christ was being tested.

It is important not to confuse personality with character. *Personality is what you display when the spotlight is on you. Character, on the other hand, is who you really are when the lights are off.* The stuff you are going through now is testing your character or maturing you the fruit in you!

Finally, to be like Christ means:

e. To maintain a fruitful life

When we speak of cloning Christ, we are essentially speaking of maintaining a fruitful life. Paul encourages us in Titus 3:14 to "live productive and fruitful lives, striving daily to do what is right and live righteously." This is cloning Christ. Again, the concept of cloning Christ can be seen in Galatians 5:22-23; the scriptures note that fruit is the direct result of the work of the Holy Spirit in a believer's heart. This manifestation of fruit allows us to display the character of Christ.

Thankfully, the fruit that the Holy Spirit gives is never out of season and always manifests itself in at least eight characteristics — in the form of love, joy, peace, kindness, goodness, faithfulness, and self-control. However the fruit manifests itself it is all the by-product of Christ's control over our lives. Subsequently, if we desire fruit to grow in us, we must connect with Christ.

In 2 Peter 1:8 Peter echoes Paul's command when he remarks, "Make every effort to add to your faith goodness, and to goodness knowledge of Christ, and to your knowledge self-control, and to self-control perseverance, and to perseverance godliness, and to godliness brotherly kindness, and to brotherly kindness, love. For if you possess these qualities in increasing measure, they will keep you from being ineffective and unfruitful..."

Singles, it is as though, God has allowed us to see the actual DNA strand for maintaining Christ-likeness. Therefore, as you endeavor to live for Christ, take inventory on not only the amount of fruit you are producing in your life but also the quality of the fruit being produced. Ask yourself, who are you looking more and more like, the world or your daddy?

Love Handles: Name five positive things about your personality, physical appearance, spiritual walk, mental capacities, and gifts/talents. Celebrate these on a regular basis!

Chapter 2

One Incident: The Danger of Having a Past

—ɯɯ—

I Corinthians 6:11 — *And that is what some of you were. But you were washed, you were sanctified, you were justified in the name of the Lord Jesus Christ and by the Spirit of our God.*

Okay, let me put it all on the table for everyone to see. The truth about our lives is this; we all have a history. There, I said it! Whether single or married, male or female, young or old, saved or sinner, black or white, Asian or Hispanic, we all have a PAST! Indeed, as different as we all are, there is at least one common thread that binds us in the same cloak of life—we all have a "Used To". I used to be this; I used to do that; I used to think this; I used to say that. No matter how old we are or how young in Christ we feel, there was a time we did not know Christ.

Nonetheless, what makes our commonness unique is that our histories are all as different as the print on a thousand snowflakes. In other words, your history or your story is different from my history or my story. There is no escaping the fact that we all have a past. Fortunately, our incidental past cannot define who we are. Furthermore, our past definitely does not have the license or authority to determine who we will become.

When Paul wrote to the Corinthian church, he was addressing people much like us who had messed up in life at least once! Because sin is so devastating and deadly, it plays for keeps and seeks to destroy what God has invested in us. Sin seeks to tear down what God has built in us. And, some of our most sinful acts put a permanent label upon our souls. In so doing, the enemy hopes to pronounce an indictment upon our future.

Paul lists a host of sins in I Corinthians; 16 – "Be not deceived: neither fornicators, nor idolaters, nor adulterers, nor the effeminate, nor abusers of themselves with mankind, nor thieves, nor the covetous, nor drunkards, nor revilers, nor extortionists shall inherit the kingdom of God." (KJV) That is quite a list of sinners. The list names sinners who sin against themselves, against others, and against God. That pretty much covers all of us. In other words, we have all fallen from time to time. Proverbs 24:16 states, "For a just man falleth seven times, and riseth up again…" (KJV). That is fact! Unfortunately, many singles have fallen and cannot get up. On the contrary, others have taken hold of God's reassurance and are able to get up each time they fall. If I were preaching this chapter, I would entitle it, "I've fallen but I can get up!"

Falling can be a good thing. Recall when the Holy Spirit fell upon the disciples in the upper room like tongues of fire upon their souls. Nothing compares to the look of a young boy who falls in love with whom he deems is the most beautiful girl in the sixth grade. Yet some falls are disastrous. Perhaps the most devastating fall occurred when Adam sinned and all of mankind fell from grace to sin.

This is not a chapter about how **to keep from falling**. We already know how to walk upright and avoid obstacles.

It is not a chapter about the **consequences of falling.** We know that the wages of sin is death. This chapter is about the love of God that enables us as Christians to **get up** each time we fall! Most assuredly, I know that God can **keep us from** falling. The scriptural prayer given in Jude 24 says, "now unto him who is able to keep us from falling..."). Yes, I know God loves us in spite of our falls. I want to prove that God's power is able to help us get up after we have fallen. This is how powerful the love of God is toward you and me.

Since we have been walking this Christian walk, some of us have experienced a spiritual upgrade. We do not fall in the areas that we used to, nor do we fall as many times as we used to fall. Our soul blemishes each time we fall in sin. Every time we entertain thoughts that should not be given center stage or speak words we should not utter even in private, we cause our spirit man to fall. Even putting our hands in places they do not belong could produce unwanted consequences for our soul. Seems at times the more we try to do right, the more we fall in sin.

According to the text, a righteous man falleth seven times, but he rises again. It looks as though the scripture is saying that we need to make sure our falling-down times never exceed our getting-up times. In other words, we should get up more times than we fall down! It is not our **fall ability** that defines us, but our **getup ability** that really determines who we are. What do we do when we fall short of what God intends? Well, I believe there are at least three steps we need to make whenever we sin. Our first step can be found in Romans 3:23 – "For all have sinned and fall short of the glory of God."

Here are three steps to make.

**Step 1 RECOGNIZE THAT YOU HAVE FALLEN —
Romans 3:23** "For **ALL** have sinned and fall short of the
glory of God." This week I have already missed the mark
and sinned several times. This morning, you messed up in
some way. Yesterday, we all fell short and sinned against
God. I am not in denial, obviously. And, just in case you are
in denial about your state of sin, remember that John writes,
"if we say we have no sin, we are deceiving ourselves." For
ALL have sinned and fallen short of God's glory.

**Step 2 CONFESS THAT YOU HAVE FALLEN AND
NEED GOD'S HELP** — Romans 3:24 states, "We are
justified freely by God's grace through the redemption that
is in Christ Jesus." As a result, we are forgiven when we
CONFESS our sins. The word "confess" means to admit
your sin and agree with God about your wrong doing. Your
appeal to God is for His mercy. When we confess our sins, I
John 1:8 tells us that God is "faithful and righteous to forgive
our sins and to cleanse us from all unrighteousness." God's
forgiveness is an act of "sending the sin away" or "dismissing
it altogether." Glory to God!

If you do not understand anything else in this chapter,
please know that your past does not have to intimidate you.
Believe it or not, it will show up at your front door from
time to time. The past loves to drop unfriendly reminders
about what used to be. Even though our past has purpose, we
do not have to remain threatened by it. The purpose of our
past is far-reaching. What would your character look like if
it were not for the strength that came from dealing with the
dirty past? I am not sure you would house the convictions
you hold so dear to your heart were it not for the stuff you
have had to endure in the past.

Maybe the rhetoric of a purposeful past and power over your sin state is not what you wanted to hear at this time. Just maybe, you have become paralyzed and ineffective in your ministry because of past sins. When the reminder of your past becomes more than you can bear, it is in your best interest to look to Jesus Christ for refuge. Look to Christ because he is our lawyer; he is the one in heaven pleading our case before God. When we acknowledge our sinful state, then repent of our wrongdoings, and trust in the mercy and saving power of Jesus Christ, he gives us the strength to get up after each fall.

During Bible study on one occasion, I recall using the demonstration of an ink blotted dress shirt to demonstrate God's grace. The white shirt had been soaked with black ink on the sleeve. As I held the shirt in the air, I asked them, "What do you see?" None of them responded as I hoped they would. Instead, all of them chimed in, "A black spot!" "But, what about the white shirt? Is there anyone who sees a white shirt," I asked? Oddly enough, none of them thought to recognize the white shirt. They only focused on the black spot on the sleeve of the shirt. This simple spot had clouded the audience's perception. There was a shirt that many were failing to recognize as the big picture.

Falls and tainted pasts leave stains on us that many people recognize years after the act of sin was committed. Singles, what do you do when the black stains of your past leave blemishes on your soul that cause others to label you according to what you used to be or used to do? There are several directions to take to rid yourselves of stained pasts, but only one is a viable option.

Many dress their sins up and attempt to disguise what they really are, but no matter how much the stain is dressed up, it remains in place. You can call it technical entertainment, but porno is porno! You can label it as recreational smoking, but marijuana is still marijuana. You may see it as expressive language, but swearing is still considered swearing. You may even view it as a natural God given stimulation, yet sexual promiscuity is still sexual promiscuity by any other name. Some singles attempt to dress it up and mask it under a different term, but the stain remains.

Some Singles, on the other hand, pretend that the stain is not really there. It is like pretending that there are no other people on earth but you. Yet, pretend as you may, the fact is that there are over a billion people on earth at this very moment. I love the illustration of the pink elephant in the living room. The drawing depicts a family going about their normal daily affairs of cleaning, reading the paper, and eating at the dinner table. All the while, a pink elephant is resting in the middle of the living room floor with a small area rug draped over its back. The family has somehow adjusted well to pretending the elephant does not exist. Much in the same way, our past is exactly as it occurred. So, pretending that it never happened is not the proper way of effectively dealing with the past.

The best remedy for a blemished past is to apply the blood of Christ to it! You think that SHOUT gets the stain out. SHOUT is nothing in comparison to the blood of Christ. The blood of Christ covers a multitude of sins and blots out our transgressions. This is what God's love does for us. When David cries out to God to "create in me a clean heart and renew a right spirit in me," he was asking God to take away the effect of the past upon his soul. II Corinthians 5:17 tells us that "if anyone is in Christ, he is a new creation; the old man has gone and behold the new man has come." When this occurs, we all become as white shirts without defects in God's sight. He no longer sees the stains once left by sin.

Step 3 – Get Up!
Just as Jesus instructed the young damsel in Mark 5:41 – "Little girl, I say to you, get up!" After you have acknowl-

edged your fall and repented of your sin, then it is time to RISE! It is time to move on with your life, your pursuits, and your service. It is time o GET UP! Because of God's plan of mercy and grace, singles are no longer defined by the events of their past. One incident no longer has any authority over your future.

Love Handles: Are there any sins you committed in the past that seem to follow you and attempt to define your character? Have you forgiven yourself for committing the sin(s)? Do you feel any of your sins are unforgivable in God's sight?

Chapter 3

Experiencing a 180

—ᵕᴧᴧᴧᵕ—

Mark 5:15-17 — *When they came to Jesus, they saw the man who had been possessed by the legion of demons, sitting there, dressed and in his right mind; and they were afraid. Those who had seen it told the people what had happened to the demon-possessed man—and told about the pigs as well. Then the people began to plead with Jesus to leave their region.*

As Jesus was getting into the boat, the man who had been demon-possessed begged to go with him. Jesus did not let him, but said, "Go home to your family and tell them how much the Lord has done for you and how he has had mercy on you." Hence, the man went away to the Decapolis, a confederacy of ten ancient cities mostly populated by Gentiles. There he began to tell how much Jesus had done for him, and all the people were amazed.

Then Jesus left the vicinity of Tyre and went through Sidon, down to the Sea of Galilee and into the region of the Decapolis. When Christ arrived at the country of the Gadarenes, he was immediately confronted with a possessed man who had been cutting himself and crying out. Throughout the first part of chapter 5, Mark takes the time to discuss this maniac. Soon, however, the maniac becomes a miracle! This once crazed person experiences a supernatural phenomenon and suddenly finds himself on a mission for Christ!

As believers we should never underestimate the power of Christ in turning individuals lives around. Just when we have given up on them, Christ is able to affect a complete turnaround in their lives. By the time we meet up with Christ and this once maniac man, we find him not on a tirade but, ironically, sitting down calm, cool, and collected. In fact, the Bible makes it clear that this man was sitting, clothed, and in his RIGHT mind. His present state was completely opposite his former. Christ had turned this man's life around for God's glory.

Interestingly enough, the Bible records that the People were afraid! I guess they had grown accustomed to this man's state of mind and surmised that he was more of a danger to himself than to others. Now, however, his current condition was a threat to them. Just minutes ago, this man was possessed by over 2,000 demons. Yet Christ commands these demons to come out of him and enter the swine of the countryside of Gerasenes. These now demon-possessed swine run, jump from a cliff, and drown in the sea.

Afterwards, the former maniac begs to go with Jesus; however, verse 19 reveals that Jesus instead sends him home on an evangelistic mission to tell his family how much the Lord has done for him and how he has shown mercy on him on this day. In previous time Christ informs those he heals, delivers, and sets free to remain discreet. Now, on the contrary, he informs this Gentile to witness to others and spread the good news of Christ and his power. What was the difference?

Let us understand something. The difference is that this one man opened up the possibility of salvation for many. In verse 20 of this same chapter, we find this same man testifying throughout all of Decapolis. This should remind us that there is no place that God's people are not present to influence. Whether in a palace or a prison, God's Word will be heard. This man ended up evangelizing throughout the entire Decapolis region.

This former maniac was not your conventional church member—he did not have a lot of fluff and rhetoric with confusing exegesis and hermeneutical expressions. He just simply told the story of what Jesus had done for him. And, to everyone he met whether Jew or Gentile, he told of how he was once in the grips of Satan, but a man named Jesus set him free!

Just like this man, many singles are bursting with testimonies of God's healing, deliverance, and provision. Moreover, we have all been in situations that required the intervening hand of God. And, if God had not stepped in when He did, we would still be on a path headed to hell with no brakes on board. Yet God, in his wisdom and love, decided to be gracious and merciful. And, he literally picked us up and turned us completely around.

Singles, I know you thought you were in control of your destiny and probably have fooled yourself into thinking that you are in complete control of your walk even now. But, a closer look would reveal a different story. If you only knew all from what God was keeping and guiding you, you would be paralyzed. God is holding you up and orchestrating your lives for his Glory. He's got you...he has me...he's got us right where he needs us to be.

When learning to walk, my son often times would run at top speeds across our living room floor. But, he was only able to stay upright because I was holding his arms up above his head. There is no way you and I would be able to navigate through the stuff in front of us or the things sent by the enemy to destroy us if it were not for the hand of the father holding us up and guiding us.

Your turned-around lives prove a couple of things:

1. There is no circumstance, situation, problem, or event greater than God's power. God is bigger than your storms and larger than your issues. Even your shortcomings are no match for God's divine order. This is important to know and believe because there will be life battles that appear to be beyond God's reach. Nevertheless, the truth is that every life event is orchestrated by the hand of God; either he fashions it or allows it. Either way, it has his signature all over it. And, because He is aware of the event and its outcome, you can rest in knowing that your souls are safe in the arms of God.

2. Likewise, God moves in the lives of men and women who have been torn up by circumstances or tormented because of choices. When God moves in the lives of trapped men and women, the first thing he does is relieve the burden and guilt. *Put it down, sister!* He has already forgiven you. *Stop picking the guilt back up, my brother!* Allow God to relieve the weight of the burden and guilt on your shoulders. God will relieve and will restore the places in your hearts, souls, and minds that were affected by the pain of your pasts. Furthermore, after he has relieved and restored you, allow God to redirect you. Only God can focus you to carry the message of hope to others, declaring to a dying world that God is a deliverer.

Let Christ change and challenge you. Allow Him to perform a spiritual makeover on your soul. Turn your life completely over to Him and allow Him to restructure, redirect, refocus, and remake you into a new creation.

Love Handles: Share with someone this week what God has done for you! Begin at home...

Chapter 4

I Can't Believe
You're Still Single!

—w—

Psalm 78:63 *"Fire consumed their young men, and their maidens had no wedding songs."*

Matthew 22:30 *"At the resurrection, people will neither marry nor be given in marriage; they will be like the angels in heaven."*

Talk to singles in your circle and you are bound to run into a few who have a list of reasons why they are still single. This chapter attempts to explain the fallacy behind some of these reasons.

#1 I am still single because of my PAST

You may be thinking that your past is too ugly and that no one would want you for a soul mate if they knew how you used to be or what you used to do. We would all be single if we bought into the mentality that no one would want us because of our past. Some of the things that happened in our lives were through no fault of our own (e.g. child molestation, rape, neglect, and so on). Other past events were the direct result of our bad choices or misguided decisions (e.g. financial bankruptcy, drug use, unhealthy relationships.). Without the grace of God, we really would not have a hope in this world.

Allow me to share something with you. If God has forgiven you and reconciled you to himself, then it falls on others to accept what God has already done. I John 1:1-10 states, "If we confess our sins to him, he is faithful and just to forgive us and to cleanse us from every wrong." (NLT) So, if there are people in your life who cannot accept the forgiveness and restoration that God has imputed upon you, then I recommend that you reevaluate your relationship with them. I have learned this about people and their perceptions of me. How they feel about me does not change how I really am. If what you think of me is true, then it still does not change anything about who I am nor how I am. If what people think of me is not true, it still does not effect who I really am and fails to change how I am. Therefore, I refuse to waste precious time entertaining others' thoughts of me. Instead, I spend my time doing at least two things. First, I have my hands full with trying to deal with my personal thoughts of who I am becoming. Secondly, during the remaining time, I spend affirming how God feels about me. When I add up the time allocated for personal reflection and spiritual reflection, I do not have the room nor the time to deal with others' perceptions.

#2 I am still single because of my family Priorities

If your extended family is currently your priority, you are to be commended. Family is perhaps the most important yet most neglected facet of our society. Do not ever stop doing what is important to you for the sake of having someone by your side. The person who enjoys your company will need to understand that family is always first. Part of finding someone with whom to spend the rest of your life is finding someone who accepts those things that you value. If you value family time, then seek someone who would welcome that same passion.

Come to think about it, I do not know of too many men who would not delight in finding someone who valued the institution of family. What woman would not want a man who knows how to take care of her when she is down? If you possess this attribute, you will need to retain this quality and not be ashamed of it. There is someone out there who would benefit greatly.

#3 I am still single because of my Post years

You may have the mindset that at your age (30, 40, 50, even 60) that the pickings are slim. If the choices are limited, it is certainly not solely because you fall into a particular age group. There are so many other factors to consider besides age. Regardless to your age, consider the percentage of singles that are truly available for a monogamous and serious relationship. Consider that few people are looking to spend their life with someone who does not know what they want out of life. Most are looking for a person who has learned to value life. You have had the opportunity to sample life and learn to prioritize the things that matter most in life. This stability is extremely beneficial in any relationship, marital or dating.

I waited until I was thirty-nine to proceed to the altar. At the age of thirty-six, I had pretty much resolved in my spirit that God had destined me for a life of celibacy. There was no one in the picture, and it seemed natural to segue from nearly twelve years of abstinence into a lifetime of singleness. I, too, had settled in my mind that no one would want to marry a nearly forty year old, graying man. Boy, was I wrong!

#4 I am still single because of my Profession

Yeah, yeah…the job you have requires too much of your time. While you break your back and rack your brain after hours to impress the boss, others are at home enjoying down time and bonding with their families. Do not misunderstand me, please; your commitment is, at best, admirable. However, as a recovering workaholic, let me warn you against placing so much importance on something that is not only unpredictable but also unstable. I know you would like to believe that your career will be there for you always, but the truth is, you really cannot count on you job. For that reason, to put it as priority over your social, spiritual, and physical needs is simply ludicrous.

No mistaking, I am glad to hear you have a career and not just another fly by night job. A career denotes accomplishment. However, do not lose sight of what God says should be your priority. The scripture says…*The unmarried woman careth for the things of the Lord, that she may be holy both in body and spirit ...* "*1 Corinthians 7:34.* Your main concern as a single Christian is serving God with your whole heart, mind, body, and soul. You will find your life so much more fulfilling if you reprioritize according to scripture.

#5 I am still single because of my Pain

Maybe, you have been down the road to marriage before and did not like the ride. Your motto became, "Burn me once, shame on you…burn me twice, shame on me." I understand and hear you clearly—you do not want to be hurt again. I understand your rationale. No one likes the feeling of being hurt. You have a right to be angry, but you do not have permission to be bitter. Anger is inevitable; bitterness is optional. You can recover from anger, but it is difficult to overcome bitterness.

I remember eating green apples from my grandmother's tree in the country. Occasionally, I would luck upon a juicy apple only to find that a worm was enjoying the juice in the apple as much as I was. Angry, I would often toss the apple to the ground. However, the next day (often shortly afterwards) I found myself climbing that same tree for another apple. I recovered from my anger to pick for another day. If I were bitter, I probably would have chosen never to eat another apple again.

Believe it or not, that is how some treat their relationships that end in a breakup. They harbor anger and bitterness in their hearts by having nothing to do with the opposite sex. It has been said that bitterness kills the soul of an individual. So, to illustrate this concept, bitterness is equivalent to pouring acid on oneself while waiting on the other person to burn. All the while, the acid of bitterness is eating away at the heart of the individual holding all that resentment inside them.

Mid-Reflection: Pray this prayer with me. Lord, help me to not harbor hatred, resentment, strife, or revenge towards anyone, especially those of past relationships. Instead, show me your ways and help me to walk in love. Release me, Father, from the bondage of my past and anoint me to press toward the mark of the high calling in Christ Jesus. Only you know the true pain and bitterness I have felt towards some. Now, God, I'm petitioning your throne of grace to move me from being bitter to being better. I love you and thank you in the name of Jesus Christ—AMEN.

#6 I am still single because of my Preoccupation with myself

True, you may just be too selfish to share your life with someone else. Boy, this one hits home! Selfishness is not a healthy mindset to have neither as a single person nor as a married couple. For thirty-eight years, I became comfortable with doing for me. If I wanted to treat myself to dinner, I did it without a blink. If it was a trip, a new suit, a concert, it was mine for the asking. When I proposed to my fiancé´ and realized that she would be moving-in six months later, I had to clean out the closets to make room for a lifetime partner and consider her whenever there was a trip planned or a concert happening. Things had changed. There was no more room for Mr. Selfish. Likewise, there is no room for selfishness in a marital relationship. So, you may be onto something here when you say that your reason for being single is because you are holding on to your selfish side.

#7 I am still single because of my Picky selection criteria
Biblically speaking, you have a right to be "selective" in your choice of a soul mate. Deuteronomy 22:9-10 warns, "Do not plant two kinds of seed in your vineyard; if you do, not only the crops you plant but also the fruit of the vineyard will be defiled. Do not plow with an ox and a donkey yoked together. The advice in the scripture is plain and easily understood. An ox and an ass have two different agendas and temperaments. While the ox is patient and focused on the task at hand, the donkey is quite unsettled and uncooperative. If the task is to plow land, then this pair would not be a productive choice. Likewise, singles must be careful that they do not choose relations with persons who are not compatible with them.

However, you can cross the line and become excessive in your selections and preferences. It is okay to make a list of non-negotiable characteristics that you will NOT accept in a soul mate, but make certain you similarly make a list of negotiable characteristics that you WILL consider. Both lists are important because they tell you more about yourself than about your potential soul mate.

When I first viewed the movie *Shallow Hal* in 2001, I did not have a clue that I too had become an extremely shallow person. I sat down after the movie was over and began to jot down a list of things that were definite turn offs for me. After I finished that list, I began jotting down a list of traits and features that were up for consideration. And, I found the negotiable list to be far shorter than the list of characteristics I was not willing to accept. As I matured, however, I found that my non-negotiable list began to shorten, and it was my negotiable list that grew tremendously. The more I understood my own shortcomings, the more tolerable I was of others'. What I understood, more than anything, was that being selective was acceptable. However, selectivity to the point of pickiness or shallowness was not acceptable.

#8 I am still single because of God's Purpose for me

If it is truly God's will for your life to remain single, then you have discovered one of His divine purposes for your life. The word of God states in I Corinthians 7:6-7 "I say this as a concession, not as a command. I wish that all men were as I am. But each man has his own gift from God; one has this gift, another has that." Scripturally, you are correct. God could have ordained your life to be a life of celibacy and singleness. But, just because there are no prospects at this time does not mean that you have been selected to receive this particular gift. Only through prayer and supplication will you know for certain what God's plan is for your life.

My prayer for you is for you to get to the point in life that you do not feel the need to explain to others about your state of singleness. I pray that you cease complaining about your lot in life and arrive at a place where you do not blame others for being where you are.

Love Handles: Do you think it is God's will for you to remain single for the rest of your life? Why?

Chapter 5

Lord of the RING-less

—∭—

Psalm 91:14 *"Because he loves me, " says the LORD, "I will rescue him; I will protect him, for he acknowledges my name."*

Princess cut, solitaire, pear shaped diamonds...set in platinum, white gold, yellow gold, or even fool's gold. No matter what size, color, carat, clarity, or cut, there is no other symbol of a lifetime commitment as strong as that of the RING. Engagement ring sales usually skyrocket during the month of February as eager young bachelors, convinced they have found the woman of their dreams, flock to jewelry stores in groves to purchase that perfect diamond for that special lady.

For the bachelor, the ring symbolizes the end of his life as a single man. In the words of my supervisor upon hearing of my impending marriage, "Eddie, life as you know it is about to change." Several folks warned me that the bathroom counter space that once provided a neat display for my hygienic supplies would no longer belong to me. I was told that all of my bachelor ways would have to be completely thrown out the window. And, you know something? They were all correct. Life for me did change. But, what several

47

people fail to realize about marriage is that it changed for the better. My life has been more enriched.

For the bachelorette, however, a ring represents the beginning of a future she has always imagined. Countless times she has envisioned what life would be like as a wife and as a mother. Would she be the best helpmate for her husband and the most nurturing mother to her children? Would her family call her blessed and see her as a virtuous woman of God?

Contrarily, for thousands of singles, February 14 serves as a reminder that they are without a mate. Whether widowed, divorced, or never married, some singles equate their ring less hands with hopeless lives. However, a ring less hand does not symbolize a hopeless life.

Perhaps, you have "never been married" or you have been the recipient of empty promises for so long that you refuse to even accept the faithful promises of God. Or, if you are divorced, maybe you have held on to hopeful expectations of someday being happily married. Again, only to repeatedly have your dreams dashed upon the jagged rocks of failed relationship after failed relationship. Even if you are widowed, you may struggle with the thought of beginning another relationship after losing the one with which you once connected for years. In spite of your situation, be reassured that there is a greater purpose for these times of ring less fingers and unfulfilled moments.

First, understand that God is not only Lord of those who are married with rings but also Lord of those without rings who are single. As Lord of the RINGS and Lord of the RINGLESS, God knows all too well the direction our life is headed. He knows which of us have been gifted with celibacy, ordained to remain unmarried for life. And, he is aware of those who have been predetermined to marry. In either case, the reality that God is more in control of what goes on in our lives than we realize is at first a difficult pill to swallow. But, when we come to fully trust Christ as Lord of our life, there is a certain peace and contentment that over-whelms us. It is the type of peace that provides a comfort in times of uncertainty – a comfort that reassures us that "all things will work together" in the end.

Realize that there is value in what God has placed in us. In a way, we are God's personal jewelry—His rings, His craftsmanship; His creation; His Bling! Well, maybe that particular way of interpreting God's word is a bit of stretch. However, in Isaiah 43:7, the word does state, "Even every one that is called by my name: for I have created him for my glory, I have formed him; yeah, I have made him." So, in other words, we have really been handcrafted by the Master. Furthermore, we all know that handcrafted items are more valuable than manufactured objects.

Ephesians 2:10 states "For we are God's workmanship, created in Christ Jesus unto good works, which God hath before ordained that we should walk in them." No one, no man, no woman, no person can give us value. We are already unique and special. So, marriage will require another special and unique individual to complement us. For now, however, our main concern is to just SHINE! God delights in showing us off to the heavens and earth. Be a single that shines for God's glory. Besides, any qualified jewelry collector is concerned with the four C's of choosing a diamond – color, cut, carat, and clarity. The combination of these four qualities helps determine the character and the value of a diamond. Any internal blemishes including cracks, black mineral deposits, or poor cutting or polishing could result in the decreased value of a diamond.

But, while jewelers specialize in finding flawless diamonds, God specializes in correcting flaws. He knows you and I are not perfect apart from him. God, therefore, desires to develop our commitment to Him, the character in each of us, and the confidence we have in Christ. Show me a Christian single that is sanctified, set apart, set-free, and satisfied in Him, and I will show you an individual walking in divine favor! Our lives shine brilliantly because of His grace.

Finally, in the midst of waiting for Mr. or Ms. Right to put an end to your pity party, you should work at developing a stronger character. I have spoken with a few single females who have their rings and dresses already picked out but who cannot seem to find the men to match. They suffer from what I call "A Case of Ringworm." Their ring finger itches right at the spot they long to have a ring placed. Please know that the world does not end just because you are not married yet.

My brothers and sisters, your lives are too precious to allow the absence of a ring to paralyze you. By all means, avoid the infectious mindset of RINGWORM. Many suffer from ringworm because they are craving the intense desire to have a wedding ring placed on their finger before it is too late! Ringworm can cause a single person to make bad decisions regarding relationships. It can cause a married person to have a lifetime of regret that they tied the knot with the wrong person. More importantly, during those ring-less moments, take the time to address these areas of your life.

1. Spiritually – Get it together! Be consistent in your prayer life as well as with the time you set aside for studying and worship. I Peter 2:2 states, "Like newborn babies, crave pure spiritual milk, so that by it you may grow up in your salvation..." Some of us have been on the formula too long...it's time to eat at the table! Pick up your Bible and study "to present yourself to God as one approved" (2 Timothy 2:15).

2. Physically – Get it together! You know what your limitations are. Push away from the table; push up from the bed and get active doing something. God needs a healthy soldier! If you cannot say Amen to that, then I will say it for you. AMEN. It is time to

get physically active! Chart some goals for yourself and begin making strides towards realizing those goals. Whether your goal is weight loss management, lowered blood pressure, or toned muscle gain, the end results begin with a decision on your part to make a change.

3. Mentally/Emotionally – Get it together and Get over it, get over him, or get over her! God wants us to operate in a renewed mindset. Romans 12:2 says, "And be not conformed to this world: but be yet transformed by the renewing of your mind, that ye may prove what is that good, and acceptable, and perfect will of God." The way you used to think and the emotional roller coaster you used to ride is over! Get off the ride because there are other attractions at the park. It is time to walk in total deliverance and no longer in partial grace.

4. Financially –Support the ministries. If the Word is blessing you, the fellowship of the membership is encouraging you, and the praise is uplifting you, then your financial support should be evident. Your financial support enables the ministry to continue without restraints. Church lighting and heating bills are not paid by faith alone. It takes revenue to keep the quality of ministry exceptional.

5. Socially — Socialize within the Christian community. Singles' most precious social commodity is their relationship with other singles. Some of the choices singles make relationally are not pleasing to God. In fact, there are likely some people in our lives who are hindering our growth in Christ. Keep in mind that diamonds do not belong in the same setting as diamoniques and cubic zirconias. I refuse to lower my standards in order to raise yours. Likewise, because you are a diamond, you do not belong in the same setting

as negative people or single people going nowhere in life.

Embrace the place wherein God has you now and learn to treasure the moments of growth. As Stormie Omartian alluded to in her book <u>Just Enough Light for the Step I'm On</u>, sometimes we can become so preoccupied with the future or even with our past that we miss the true value of the PRESENT. You might be without a ring right now, but you still have someone who loves you and will always love you unconditionally – Christ Jesus. Indeed, God does declare marriage as a holy institution between a man and his wife. This is the same God that promises to return for us to receive the Church as His bride. That makes him Lord of the Rings as well as Lord of the Ring-less!

Love Handles: How important is having a ring on your finger? What would the ring symbolize? Which of the five areas do you need to spend time developing or correcting?

Chapter 6

From Prostitution to Promise: Turning back to God

—w—

Ezekiel 23:1-49 (Amplified Bible)
1-10 - God's Message came to me: *"Son of man,
there were two women, daughters of the same mother.
They became whores in Egypt, whores from a young
age. Their breasts were fondled, their young bosoms
caressed. The older sister was named Oholah, the
younger was Oholibah. They were my daughters,
and they gave birth to sons and daughters. Oholah is
Samaria and Oholibah is Jerusalem. Oholah started
whoring while she was still mine. She lusted after
Assyrians as lovers: military men smartly uniformed
in blue, ambassadors and governors, good-looking
young men mounted on fine horses. Her lust was
unrestrained. She was a whore to the Assyrian elite.
She compounded her filth with the idols of those to
whom she gave herself in lust. She never slowed
down. The whoring she began while young in Egypt
she continued, sleeping with men who played with
her breasts and spent their lust on her. So I left her to
her Assyrian lovers, for whom she was so obsessed*

with lust. They ripped off her clothes, took away her children, and then, the final indignity, killed her. Among women her name became Shame—history's judgment on her.

Ezekiel 23:1-49 is the story of two prostitutes (Aholah and Aholibah) who represent the nations of Samaria and Jerusalem respectively. When I tell you these sisters were BAD, I mean BADDDDDD! Aholah, the elder of the two, was the first to lead a very promiscuous lifestyle. The Bible says that while she was still God's daughter, she engaged in prostitution. How embarrassing it must be for a daddy to see his little girl engaging in such a demoralizing act. Yet, as demeaning as her lifestyle was and would become, God's love for her never changed.

To make matters worse, however, she was the one lusting after them. She lusted after handsome men, men of honor, dignity, enemies, and even idols! The Bible calls her a whore of unrestrained nature. She unleashed her lust upon any and every willing person or thing. Yet, God's love for her remained the same. No mistaking, God did not approve of her lifestyle. But, that is just like God. He does not approve of the sin but continues to love the sinner, nonetheless. Because God despised her sinful state more than his love for her, he left her to her own devices. In verses 9-10, we find that she has been turned over to her enemies and left to reckon with her lust on her own.

Romans 1:28 - And even as they did not like to retain God in their knowledge, God gave them over to a reprobate mind, to do those things which are not convenient.

Her Assyrian lovers had their way with her, ripping off her clothes, taking away her children, and finally killing her.

The Bible says her name means SHAME among the women of Israel, even to this day. However, the story does not end there but begins to take on another shape in the verses that follow.

In versus 11-21 it states - *Her sister Oholibah saw all this, but she became even worse than her older sister in lust and whoring, if you can believe it. She also went crazy with lust for Assyrians: ambassadors and governors, military men smartly dressed and mounted on fine horses—the Assyrian elite. And I saw that she also had become incredibly filthy. Both women followed the same path. Yet Oholibah surpassed her sister. When she saw figures of Babylonians carved in relief on the walls and painted red, fancy belts around their waists, elaborate turbans on their heads, all of them looking important—famous Babylonians!—she went wild with lust and sent invitations to them in Babylon. The Babylonians came on the run, fornicated with her, made her dirty inside and out. When they had thoroughly debased her, she lost interest in them. Then she went public with her fornication. She exhibited her sex to the world. I turned my back on her just as I had on her sister. But that did not slow her down. She went at her whoring harder than ever. She remembered when she was young, just starting out as a whore in Egypt. That whetted her appetite for more virile, vulgar, and violent lovers—stallions obsessive in their lust. She longed for the sexual prowess of her youth back in Egypt, where her firm young breasts were caressed and fondled.*

All along, in the shadows, her younger sister witnessed the demise of her older sibling. And, you would think that seeing what her sister went through would be enough to deter her from making the same wrong decisions. But, nooooooooo! Ironically, the younger sister turned around and became worse than her older sister. The Bible says she surpassed her sister's deeds, going as far to invite the Babylonians to a sex party. One interpretation says that she first saw the

Babylonians on a wall as a painted mural and went wild with lust over their pictures alone. The Babylonians, upon receiving the invitation, came running to fondle her, rape her, and dirty her inside and out. When they had done all they could to her, SHE lost interest in them. Wait a minute! She lost interest or they lost interest? The Bible is clear that SHE was the one who lost interest in the end. When God turned his back on her as he had her sister, Oholibah became worse. Her lust became more intense; she chased men who were like stallions. Let us not go there in this chapter as to what that implies; we will keep it PG-13.

God finally sends a message to let her know that her life-style would no longer be tolerated. He warned her of what was to come in her future. She would be defaced, disfigured, demoralized, and ultimately destroyed. God instructed Ezekiel to take a message to both Samaria and Jerusalem that just as these sisters would be destroyed; they too would pay for what they had allowed to take place.

Psalm 106:39 states, "They defiled themselves by what they did; by their deeds they prostituted themselves."

Because of their deeds, God issued his judgment upon them both. Their judgment was actually an indictment upon Jerusalem, which had prostituted itself among nations. Samaria and Jerusalem had paraded their lusts among heathen nations and were now longing to reunite with their first lust – Egypt.

God instructed Ezekiel's words to be convicting and convincing. The people had to know that God would make them pay for the evil they had done, especially for bringing that mess into His sanctuary. Harsh judgment had to occur so that His people and the generation to follow would know that God is the one true Sovereign God!

In versus 22-27 — *"Therefore, Oholibah, this is the Message from God, the Master: I will incite your old lovers against you, lovers you got tired of and left in disgust. I will bring them against you from every direction, Babylonians and all the Chaldeans, Pekod, Shoa, and Koa, and all Assyrians—good-looking young men, ambassadors and governors, elite officers and celebrities—all of them mounted on fine, spirited horses. They will come down on you out of the north, armed to the teeth, bringing chariots and troops from all sides. I will turn over the task of judgment to them. They will punish you according to their rules. I will stand totally and relentlessly against you as they rip into you furiously. They will mutilate you, cutting off your ears and nose, killing at random. They will enslave your children—and anybody left over will be burned. They will off your clothes and steal your jewelry. I will put a stop to your sluttish sex, the whoring life you began in Egypt. You will not look on whoring with fondness anymore nor will you think back on Egypt with stars in your eyes."*

Verse 35 — *"Therefore God, the Master, says, Because you've forgotten all about me, pushing me into the background, you now must pay for what you've done—pay for your sluttish sex and whoring life."*

Versus 48-49 — *"I'll put an end to sluttish sex in this country so that all women will be well warned and not copy you. You'll pay the price for all your obsessive sex. You'll pay in full for your promiscuous affairs with idols. And you'll realize that I am God, the Master."*

After all that has been written in this chapter, I am certain by now you are wondering what happened to the latter part of the chapter's title – Promise. If the title of this chapter had only read PROSTITUTION, there would not be much hope. However, the title reads *From Prostitution to Promise*.

Believe it or not, there is promise remaining in the book of Ezekiel. If you continue to read Ezekiel, you will read in

Chapter 36 that God never stopped loving his people. In fact, he never forgot his promise to the nation of Israel. Despite the whorish ways of His people, God's love never failed!

In Ezekiel 36, God announces through the prophet that He would sanctify His great name, take them from among the heathen, and bring them into the land he had promised them. Once the people were situated in the land, God says that he would sprinkle clean water on them and they would be cleansed from all the filthiness they had amassed.

> *Ezekiel 36:26, 29 – And I will give you a new heart, and I will put a new spirit in you...I will cleanse you of your filthy behavior.*

Because God had bigger plans for his people than they had for themselves, he held true to His promise to them.

Consequently, Singles, I admonish you to stop looking to the right-now to find satisfaction. There is so much more awaiting you according to God's plan for your life. He did not create you to prostitute with the world. You are a daddy's child who deserves his blessings through Christ Jesus. I am so glad that I serve a living God who pursues me. In spite of my inadequacies and hang-ups, God pursues me. He delights in moving from a life of Prostitution to a life of Promise!

Singles, please do not continue to break God's heart. Today, I am pleading with you to surrender to a lifestyle of holiness and holy living. Quit prostituting your gifts and serve God with your whole heart, mind, body, and soul. Give him the parts of your mind and soul that the world desires to prostitute and corrupt.

Keep in mind that God desires to see us move from people of prostitution to children of promise.

Love Handles: What does God expect from you during your single years?

Chapter 7

Never Underestimate Tomorrow!

—⚬⚬—

2 Corinthians 1:8-9 - We do not want you to be unin-
formed, brothers, about the hardships we suffered in
the province of Asia. We were under great pressure,
far beyond our ability to endure, so that we despaired
even of life. Indeed, in our hearts we felt the sentence
of death. But this happened that we might not rely on
ourselves but on God, who raises the dead.

In John 20:1-2, the writer remarks, *"Early on the first day*
of the week, while it was still dark, Mary Magdalene went
to the tomb and saw that the stone had been removed from
the entrance. So she came running to Simon Peter and the
other disciple, the one Jesus loved, and said, "They have
taken the Lord out of the tomb, and we don't know where
they have put him!" So Peter and the other disciple started
for the tomb. Both were running, but the other disciple
outran Peter and reached the tomb first. He bent over and
looked in at the strips of linens lying there but did not go in.
Then Simon Peter, who was behind him, arrived and went
into the tomb. He saw the strips of linen lying there, as well
as the burial cloth that had been around Jesus' head. The
cloth was folded up by itself, separate from the linen. Finally

the other disciple, who had reached the tomb first, also went inside. He saw and believed. (They still did not understand from Scripture that Jesus had to rise from the dead.) Then the disciples went back to their homes."

John 20 identifies one Savior – Jesus the Christ. At the same time, he reveals the nature of three minor characters - Mary Magdalene, Simon Peter, and John. Each of these three characters exhibits three different points of view. In fact, all three characters differ in the way they perceived the events of the final days leading up to the resurrection of Christ.

It was Mary who reflected on the <u>Trial of the Cross</u>. Mary is a significant character, in that; she is the person that had seven demons cast from her soul. She is also important because she had a personal encounter with Jesus the Christ and because she is the last follower to leave the site of the cross and the first one to reach the tomb on the third day. She comes to the tomb with the tragedy of days ago still on her mind.

However, Simon Peter realizes the <u>Tragedy of the Tomb</u>. Upon hearing of what Mary had witnessed, Simon and the other disciples flee to the grave site focusing on the <u>Tragedy of the Tomb</u>. Simon Peter was a fisherman by day and an apostle by night. He was the one disciple who walked on water, cut off a soldier's ears, and denied Jesus. His behavior was erratic and unpredictable. But, when it came to the days following the death of Jesus, we find Simon focusing on the tomb, the final resting place of Jesus. In fact, upon surveying the tomb's contents, the scriptures state that Peter went back home. Despite what he had been called to do and all that he had learned of Christ, he still did not quite understand that the tomb was not Jesus' final resting place. For it was written, Christ had to rise!

In contrast, it was John who decided to focus on the <u>Triumph of the Resurrection</u>. John is noteworthy given that he was an apostle and the brother of James; he is also known as the disciple whom Jesus loved. He chooses to focus not on the tragedy, nor the tomb, but on the triumph of the resurrection! John focuses on the <u>prophetic nature of Jesus' resurrection</u>, the fact that prophecy had been fulfilled and mankind had been redeemed.

These were three different people with three different perspectives on the resurrection of Jesus Christ. Much in the same way, you and I can live our lives with one of these three focuses.

The Lenses of a Tragedy

We could focus on the tragedies of life. You might even view your singleness as a tragedy. However, your singleness is not a tragedy. Of course, being married to the wrong individual is a tragedy greater than remaining single. Viewing life through the lenses of tragedy may leave you in a confused state of mind and upset your perceptions. Thus, you should stop focusing on tragedies because they cheat you of your victory.

The Lenses of the Tomb

Singles, you should also stop focusing on the tombs of life. Focusing on the tombs of life is not a healthy approach either. Mainly because dead things can occupy the time you should spend serving God. Also, stop allowing the dead things in life such as dead relationships or dead dreams take you away from what God called you to do. I know it is easy to view your last relationship as a tomb situation or hopeless, but the truth is that many have abandoned us at different points in our lives. And, when they left us, they likely thought that it was the final chapter. But, had they kept reading, they would have discovered that in the next chapter God added a bit of irony. Perhaps, they thought they had put you in the grave, but God had another plan in mind for your life. People who went through what Christ endured died one hundred percent of the time. But, what many failed to realize is that earlier in the scriptures, Jesus declared that he was the Resurrection.

You may be asking, what is resurrection? Resurrection means literally to rise from a dead situation; there is no way it can be put down for the final count! The very nature of the resurrection is its ability to get up when knocked down. The next time folks write you off and consider you destroyed and hopeless, tell them, "Just give me a few days; God has a way of turning things around!"

The Lenses of John

We could all go through life and view our circumstances through the lenses of John. By this, I mean that we could focus on the triumph of the resurrection. The resurrection of Christ is vital to the entire system of faith Christians believe and practice. If Christ had not arisen, then our faith is in vain and the whole of humanity is lost forever. But, thank God Christ got up and declared all power.

History reports that during the Battle of the Waterloo, a man stood on top of a great cathedral in London. Like an aircraft carrier who holds signal flags, the man stood for hours waving signal flags with a message about the battle between the Duke of Wellington and Napoleon. Everyone in the entire city of London anxiously waited to know how things were going. The man stood on that cathedral watching for signals from the battlefield and relayed this news to the onlookers below. When he received a final message he waved his flags to give the people of London a report on the battle. When the people of London looked up they could barely see the message being waved through the thick fog. The message they were able to see was, "Wellington defeated." They could not believe it. Their hearts sank much like the hearts of those who loved Christ and witnessed his death and burial.

But then there came a break in the fog and they saw the rest of the message that said, "Wellington defeated Napoleon." The entire nation of England rejoiced much like John must have rejoiced at the thought of the resurrection promise.

When Jesus died, the message that came to the disciples' heart was, "Jesus defeated." When Jesus died it was a moment of sadness. Yet, three days later, the fog cleared, and the message they received was, "Jesus defeated Satan." When He rose from the dead, it was a moment of triumph and victory! Christians around the world celebrate the glorious truth that Jesus Christ arose from the dead and is alive. Thank God we serve a Sunday morning God who would not let Friday tell it all! Friday told of a suffering man, but Sunday announced a Risen Savior. Thank God we serve a God who still moves stones!

When you look at the condition of your life, you may feel like it is Friday and you are on the cross. Or, possibly, life's circumstances may have you feeling like it is Saturday and you are dead and gone. But, I would hope there are some who have turned their outlook completely around and see themselves at the morning of their resurrection! Never underestimate tomorrow, even if yesterday was a trial and today seems hopeless. Christ is still in charge – he holds tomorrow in His hand.

Love Handles: Share a resurrection moment in your life—a point in life when you had been counted out for good, but GOD raised you to newness in life.

Section 2

Over Exposure

—⁓—

Worlds Apart
By E. Marcel Jones

Our worlds, though in the same solar system,
Are worlds apart – two worlds so far
That I see your stars and wonder where you are

I feel as if I can reachhhhh out
And capture each one in my palms
But, I can't because our worlds are worlds apart

I could climb aboard a rocket ship
and land on your surface
But, it would be so much quicker
To catch a shooting star going in your direction

Oh, to feel your atmosphere, to explore your terrain
I wonder would a collision bring us together
Or, would it destroy what we already have

I could easily step out of my usual orbit
And the gravitational pull alone
Would bring me within light years of your path

But, for now, to keep with the order
That's been predetermined
I'll remain content with our distance

Content…though we're worlds apart
Two worlds really close, yet so far

Chapter 8

Seven Deadly Sins of Singles

—ɷ—

Romans 6:21 — *What benefit did you reap at that time from the things you are now ashamed of? Those things result in death!*

W hether you are divorced, widowed, or never married, the common thread that weaves you all on one accord is that you have been singled out! You have been singled out for God's glory. God has you right where he wants and needs you at this particular point in your life. Until you come to grips with this fact, you will forever find yourself wandering in the wilderness of your pity party in search of someone to rescue you and meet you at the altar. Not that the idea of marriage is impossible for you, but what God wants you to understand is that there is a greater purpose behind where you are now. God desires that you seek those things that bring him glory and not be overly concerned with other things.

Anxiety over getting married, getting older, having children may all be legitimate concerns, but none of these issues should be occupying your minds. Sweating over these things may keep you from achieving the heights to which God is trying to get you. The scripture states in Matthew 6:33, "Seek first the kingdom of heaven (God) and His righteousness and all of these things shall be added unto you." To seek God's face is to pursue His divine order and way of doing things. It literally means to seek God's purpose for your life. If you and I busy ourselves with doing this daily, we would have no room for panicking over the things we have not achieved or the items we have not amassed in life. If we set out to pursue God's way of doing things and seek out his purpose for our lives daily, the promise in the scripture is that at some point all of the other things will be added to our account!

Today, as you begin your quest, know that the enemy is noting your paradigm shift in thinking. And, while you are seeking God's kingdom and his righteousness, the enemy will be seeking you as well. He desires to preoccupy your lives with distracters. Distracters look good and maybe appear harmless in moderation, but too much of them or an abundance of them could prove quite harmful. Distracters keep us entangled and off balance. For this reason, becoming wrapped up in distracters causes a misalignment with God's purpose. And, a life not aligned with God's Word is pointless and non-productive. In order to keep from falling victim to the enemy over and over, singles must be aware of and avoid seven deadly sins.

The Seven Deadly Sins of Singles

1. Disobedience **(I Samuel 15:22) To obey is better than sacrifice, and to hearken than the fat of rams.** Disobedience of any kind is viewed as rebellion. Acting in one's own strength is as dangerous as going into a lion's den armed with nothing but a bowl of blood. Continuous disobedience kills our relationship with God. God has a way of turning rebellious hearts over to a "reprobate mind." And, if God is not on our side, who is? In your quest for God's way of doing things, never lose sight of the value of obedience. A

parent-child relationship is enriched when the child is in obedience to the parent's requests. But, the second that child steps out of line, there is tension in the relationship with the parent. Therefore, the first sin to avoid is disobedience. One sure way of avoiding the sin of disobedience is to stop listening to what the enemy says about God's will for your life.

2. Sexual Promiscuity **(I Corinthians 3:16-17) Know ye not that you are the temple of God, and that the Spirit of God dwelleth in you? (KJV)** Sexual Promiscuity destroys our temple. There will be more in later chapters regarding this area. For now, just know that this sin is detrimental to the health of our soul.

3. Selfishness **(Philippians 2:4) Look not every man on his own things, but every man also on the things of others. (KJV)** Selfishness has no place in any relationship except with ones self. As the term implies, life becomes all about SELF. When a person's life is centered solely on himself/herself, the sin that enters causes his or her influence to sour. Selfishness kills the mission God has for us. Selfishness may be the very thing that is holding us back from God's promises. Before I got married, I had to come to grips with the amount of selfishness that existed in my life. I prided myself on being a selfless person but soon realized through conviction from several important people in my life that I was SELFISH. I thought looking out for me was considered self-concern, not selfishness. I Corinthians 10:24 states, "Nobody should seek his own good, but the good of others."

Galatians 6:2 adds, "Carry each other's burdens, and in this way you will fulfill the law of Christ."

4. Hypocrisy **(James 1:22) But be ye doers of the word, and not hearers only, deceiving your own selves.** Hypocrisy kills our witness. **Matthew 23:27-28** warns, "Woe to you, teachers of the law and Pharisees, you hypocrites! You are like whitewashed tombs, which look beautiful on the outside but on the inside are full of dead men's bones and everything unclean. In the same way, on the outside you appear as righteous, but on the inside you are full of hypocrisy and wickedness." Romans 2:1 voices, "You, therefore, have no excuse, you who pass judgment on someone else, for at whatever point you judge the other, you are condemning yourself, because you who pass judgment do the same things."

5. Anger/Wrath **(Ephesians 4:26) Be ye angry and sin not; let not the sun go down upon your wrath v. 27 neither give place to the devil. (KJV)** Anger and wrath kill our brethren. Proverbs 22:24 advises, "Do not make friends with a hot-tempered man; do not associate with one easily angered." Ephesians 4:31 adds, "Get rid of all bitterness, rage, and anger, brawling and slander, along with every form of malice."

6. Love of Money (I Timothy 6:10) **For the love of money is the root of all kinds of evil. Some people, eager for money, have wandered from the faith and pierced themselves with many griefs.** No matter how much wealth a person accumulates, the wealth is not worth loving. Certainly, there is no question that money can purchase many things, but that does not make it worth loving. The trap of loving money has a vice grip that is not easily escapable. Once this sin takes root it affects everything it comes in contact with, including a person's job, family, church, and body.

Luke 9:25 asks the question, "What good is it for a man to gain the whole world, and yet lose or forfeit his very self"? How appropriate a question this is, especially for a single man or woman willing to sacrifice all that is righteous just to have attained money. It is simply not worth the end result to have a love for money. Does this mean that singles should not strive to earn a decent living or purchase luxury items according to their tastes? Certainly not! The Bible is explicit in its instructions to holy people of God to not put money above God. Rich men have existed since Father Abraham, but the people of God should be careful not to worship money.

The love of money can kill our wealth. In fact, money cannot determine my true wealth. My wealth as a person is determined first of all by the value that God places upon me. He created me. That means I have been touched by the hand of God; this places a huge value on my life. Secondly, God has deposited gifts of infinite value in my spirit to be used to serve Him. Each gift is worth more than gold because it has an eternal effect on all I come in contact with on earth. Finally, the blood of God's Son, Christ Jesus, has been applied to my soul and makes me priceless! Proverbs 11:4 – Wealth is worthless in the day of wrath, but righteousness delivers from death.

7. Jealousy/Envy **(Proverbs 14:30) A heart at peace gives life to the body, but envy rots the bones.** Jealously kills our vision and can damage our self-esteem. James 3:16 - For where envying and strife is, there is confusion and every evil work. This is an area that God has to work on, not man. Allow God to keep you from comparing yourself and your life to others'.

Love Handles: How many deadly sins have you been guilty of at one time in your life? Which of these sins has the least stronghold on your spirit?

Chapter 9

From Lust Factor to Fear Factor

—ഡ—

I Corinthians 7:9 – *But if they cannot contain, let them marry: for it is better to marry than to burn.*

Paul obviously understood that the plight of singles in Biblical times would continue to be the fight of many singles in modern times. His sound advice to the church at Corinth still stands as the golden rule among singles today.

Most commentaries intimate when Paul used the term burn, he was referring to burning with passion. However, a few bold interpretations take it a step further to denote a physical burn (e.g. a painful venereal disease causing a burning sensation in the urine tract) or a spiritual burn (i.e. a connotation of eternal damnation in hell). Regardless to how you interpret this passage, the fact still remains that marrying is the better option to burning.

Taking the lead from those commentators that surmise Paul's reference was to a physical burning, I want to talk candidly in this chapter about the effects of sexually transmitted diseases upon the mind, body, and soul. My hopes are that you, the reader, will turn from any activity that does not glorify God, especially sexual activities out of the will of God. Sexual activity out of the will of God may result in more than pregnancy but may also involve contracting a sexually transmitted disease (STD). Whether through vaginal, oral, or anal intercourse, sexually transmitted diseases are serious considerations for singles engaged in pre-marital relations. With over 20 diseases transmitted sexually and some of these diseases with over 100 strains or types, it is no wonder that millions of people contract these diseases on the hour. It has been reported that twenty-five percent of all HIV cases each year are the result of people ages thirteen through twenty-one.

Some of the diseases detailed in this chapter show no signs of infection while others are so aggressive that they are fatal. With the increased use of drug use and sharing of unclean needles, a newer, broader term has recently surfaced — STI's (Sexually Transmitted Infections). Now, people may be infected through childbirth with the use of dirty IV needles or even through breastfeeding. In March of 2008, the Center for Disease Control released its findings for STD's among teenagers. In the report, it was noted that one in four teen girls (ages fourteen-nineteen) is the carrier of at least one of the most common sexually transmitted diseases. African American girls were affected at a rate of forty-eight percent compared to white teen girls at twenty percent.

In addition, the 2008 report showed that there has been a significant rise in the number of syphilis cases among all male and female homosexuals. For the past seven years, the CDC has noticed an increase in cases reported among these two groups specifically. This is further exacerbated by the increasing number of bi-sexual men who continue in their down-low lifestyles, affecting both their male and female partners. Consequently, among all adults, it was reported in 2006 that 56,300 new cases of people were infected with H.I.V. The key word is "reported." Because so many more never get tested for the disease, it is estimated that this alarming number of new cases is perhaps forty percent higher in reality. This would mean that the number of new cases in 2006 could be as high as 200,000.

It must be concluded that for singles, the best prevention is abstinence. Despite the advertisements and campaigns for condom use, the best prevention is abstinence. There is no guessing or wondering that takes place when abstinence is being practiced. Moreover, at the moment a young lady opens her door to the possibility of a sexual encounter or a young man entertains the idea of indulging in needle sharing, the possibility of contracting an STD or STI is introduced.

Below is a short list of nine diseases that abstinence could help you avoid:

Diseases (Symptoms)

- **Cancroids** (Cause painful ulcers and sores usually on the genitals)
- **Chlamydia** (For women, damage to the reproductive organs; for men, discharge from penis)
- **Hepatitis B** (Causes damage to the liver; dark urine; muscle pain; loss of appetite)
- **Herpes simplex** (Recurrent skin irritation red bumps, open sores, and blisters on genital or anal regions)
- **HIV/AIDS** (Interferes with the body's ability to fight off viruses and disease causing agents; can lead to AIDS)
- **HPV** (Can cause genital warts and lead to cervical cancer, penis cancer, oral cancer, and head cancer)
- **Gonorrhea** (Causes a painful burning feeling in urination; pus-like discharge from anus, penis, or vagina)
- **Syphilis** (Causes damage to the heart, brain, and nerves; sores on tongue or rectum; symptoms come and go)
- **Trichomoniasis** (Causes odd odor from vagina; itchy discharge)

Usually, the mucus membrane of the penis, vulva, or even the mouth is the site of transmission for many of these diseases. You may say, "Well, just put a condom on." Well indeed, there are several problems with this statement.

1st - Condoms are **NOT** 100% effective. Although they provide a barrier, most condoms provide a semi-permeable barrier. The term "semi" means that microscopic matter may still pass through, especially virus causing agents that are thousands of times smaller than sperm.

2nd - Wearing a condom too small may cause leakage; wearing a condom to large may cause slippage.

3rd - Removing the condom after ejaculation may cause spillage.

There are just too many factors to be considered for one to rely solely on a condom to prevent disease. If you really want to protect your body, let us talk about other areas that are left vulnerable. For instance, unfortunately there is no condom or protection for the MIND. After the sexual activity is complete and you are left with this feeling of being used for someone else's pleasure, it would be great if your mind was not affected. In addition, no condoms are made for the HEART. Think about the time you thought you were in love with her and she with you. Only to find out that she was in love with Jerome, Harold, and Renaldo too. Your heart may not have suffered the aches if you had had a condom for your heart.

Maybe, you needed a condom for your SOUL. You have had over ten sexual partners in the last three years. Yet, none of them asked your hand in marriage. Heck, none of them was really interested in a long-term commitment. They just wanted to get you in the beneath the sheets for a quick minute so they could say they "had you." Now that you have been had, you have ten covenants with ten different souls. You have united so many times with so many different spirits that you are technically no longer single. Each covenant was a marriage ceremony performed. It certainly would have been nice to have had a condom to protect your soul. Would it not?

This is how sexual interludes often play out: All she wanted was for him to love her and be intimate with her so that she felt loved by him. She was ready to carry his child. All he wanted was the sensation of releasing without the impartation of his seed. This story sounds similar to a man in the Bible named Onan. Even today, there are singles who suffer from what I term the "Onan Complex."

The Onan Complex occurs whenever we sacrifice rather than obey what our Daddy has instructed us to do. Onan was the second son of Judah. After his elder brother died (Er), Judah asked his son Onan to have sex with his sister-in-law Tamar. Because Tamar had not yet given birth, this was Judah's way of giving her a child and his way of declaring an heir for Er. In other words, even though Onan would have fathered the child, Judah would look at the offspring as Judah's heir. While Onan did not mind having sex with Tamar, he objected to depositing his seed into her womb if he could not declare the child as his own. Consequently, instead of ejaculating into her womb, Onan withdrew and "spilled his seed" to the ground. Because of this act of rebellion, God became displeased and killed Onan. For Onan, sex was not about making deposits but about making quick withdrawals. He delighted in the SENSATION but despised the IMPARTATION. Both characters, Tamar and Onan had goals, but one was left SATISFIED while the other was left with a VOID.

His act was not masturbation, but the act of masturbation is another example of sensation without impartation. Viewing pornographic material, something I struggled with for years in my early single years, is yet another example of sensation without impartation. Thank God for His continual deliverance. Spilling your seed into any vessel short of your wife's womb is considered sensation without impartation. Men, how many times have you enjoyed the SENSATION but despised the IMPARTATION? She was not the kind of woman with whom you wanted to have your children, but she was good enough to heighten your passions for the night. Ladies, how many times have you been the victim of sexual affair after sexual affair, hoping that one day before your egg alarm rings you would be blessed with a child?

A recent survey revealed that Americans can account for an average of about 14.5 sexual partners in a lifetime. I am certain you may know of people that have surpassed this number. Still, there may be several that are not even close to knowing double digit sexual partners. It is all about choices in the midst of temptation. What can you do if the temptation is too strong? When dealing with temptation you can either:

1. Give in to it because it feels too good to fight or
2. Fight in your own strength and lose most of the time
3. Or, overcome it through the power of the ONE who was and is victorious over sin—Christ Jesus.

Regardless to your situation, it is obvious that there is a lust factor that exists in our world — a pandemic that is gripping our communities, even church communities.

Fight manfully onward, dark passions subdue, each victory will help you, Jesus will carry you through. Ask the Savior to help you, comfort, strengthen, and keep you; He is willing to aid you, Jesus will carry you through!

Love Handles: April is STD Awareness Month. Make it your goal to know your status (HIV positive or negative) during this month. If you are dating someone, and it is becoming seriously close to a long-term commitment, it would be most beneficial if you knew his or her status as well. For more information about how you can raise the awareness of STD's in your community, visit www.cdcnpin. com/stdawareness

Chapter 10

Does size really matter?

—ᨰᨰ—

Numbers 13:32 — *And they spread among the Israelites a bad report about the land they had explored. They said, "The land we explored devours those living in it. All the people we saw there are of great size."*

Just as the Israelites considered the size of the inhabitants before they entered the Promised Land, many singles are concerned with size when looking for a mate. The question to which many want answers is, "When it comes to selecting a soul mate, does size really matter?" Single sisters in Christ want to know if body type and size matter to single brothers. Are men in search of pencil thin and pretty or curvaceous and cute? Men want to know if sisters are in search of a million-aire mogul or a minimum-wage hunk. From body size and car size to the size of one's bank account, inquiring minds would like to know if size indeed matters. As intimidating as the Israelites were upon seeing a land inhabited by people of great size, single men and women are just as intimidated by the thought of approaching someone with more than what they have. However, there are some things more important than size.

Let us examine a few:

Is this the kind of mate you are looking to find?
What qualities do you possess that will contribute to the
success of the marriage?
Has God given you permission to move in this
direction?

First, what kind of mate are you in search of at this point in your life? Whether you are looking for a Teammate or an Inmate, a Roommate or a Playmate, a Helpmate or a Soul mate, you should have a clear understanding of the type of MATE you want in matrimony. Without a clear vision of what is ideal in your life, you might end up with a MISMATE or a PRIMATE. Understand that each of these mates require different levels of commitment.

A teammate is fabulous if you are looking to win at playing games. As long as you both are winning and giving it one hundred percent, your mate may remain committed. Yet the second you start losing at the game of life, team-mates have a tendency of switching teams or worse. They may just sit on the bench while you tackle the opponent on your own. For example, Peter was a great teammate for Jesus when all was going well. Who had Christ's back in the garden and cut off the man's ear? Peter! Who walked on water towards Christ when he appeared on the sea in the middle of the night? Peter! But, who switched sides at Calvary? Peter! Thank God, we serve a forgiving coach who gives us a second chance.

Inmates are great to have if you are content with remaining in your own world without any interaction from the outside. Maybe you have no aspirations of ever moving beyond your 8 x 8 mentality. But, if you ever wrap your mind around a 20 x 40 concept, you will not find satisfaction ever again in settling for anything smaller. Never talk of escaping the mundane if you are with an inmate (no offense to my brothers and sisters in Christ who are in a physical cell block – this is just an analogy). Remember, Lot's wife was an inmate. In the midst of escaping the demise of Sodom and Gomorrah, she did the one thing they were instructed not to do – turn back. She longed for the 8 x 8 cell when God had instructed Job's family to move to a 20 x 40 inheritance. What a pity that some of us never quite achieve what God has for us because we desire to remain in the small comfort of yesterday's habitations.

Now, when it comes to one of the coolest mates around, I would have to give props to roommates. They are great at sharing and caring. Roommates provide the right amount of conversation and fun a person would ever need. The only problem is that roommates are not willing to change as you change. The older the relationship grows, the more you both begin to learn about each other. All of your bad habits begin to surface and most of their smoke screen begins to dissipate. The real person begins to take form, causing you to either conform to the change or move out. Most roommates chose to move out. This creates another liability because having roommates are mostly financial arrangements that require a lease or contract. Someone is always stuck with the lease when one decides to leave.

On the other hand, playmates are fine if you are into juvenile and immature relationships. Playmates always talk of growing up but never put it into action. There is a saying I love: "Growing old is inevitable, but growing up is optional." I love this quote because it paints the very picture of play-mates in their 40's that still act as if they are five years of age! As ridiculous as this sounds, it is reality for many singles that are locked in playmate relationships. Sure, at first it was a lot of fun — the trips, the outings, the sex, the sand at the beach, the rides at the amusement park. However, during the trip to the amusement park, the playmate may have gotten on the roller coaster ride with you, but somewhere around the twentieth time riding the Screaming Eagle, your playmate decides to get off and leaves you on alone. Now, here you are three years later, still stuck with the loops of your emotions, the twists of your tears, and the dips of your depression on a ride that your playmate abandoned years ago. You sit alone wondering if he or she will ever get back on the ride with you. If you look to the side, however, you notice that your playmate is now on the Merry Go Round with Boomshika! Or, maybe your playmate can be seen sharing cotton candy with Harold, Jimbo, or Peter without even a thought of you. Playmates are fun at first, but they are not what you need if you are looking for a long-term commitment.

When it comes to ultimate commitment, we have to focus on the remaining mates – Helpmate and Soul mate. God instructed Adam that Eve would now be his Helpmate. She would be known as his Soul mate because she was created from him and for him. You are a blessed man of God when you find your Helpmate and Soul mate. Nothing completes you more than locating the person who has what you are missing! Unlike the aforementioned Mates, when it comes to Helpmates and Soul mates, size does NOT matter. Do not get me wrong, a sizeable bank account is great to have, but it is not the determining factor for finding your Soul mate. In fact, a sizeable home, huge salary, or even enormous ego has no relevance to the Helpmate. The most important factor with which Soul mates are concerned is the quality of their relationship with Jesus Christ.

Is your faith small, inconspicuous, and ineffective? Or, do you possess the kind of great faith that moves mountains. A soul mate is not concerned with the size of your hands and feet but more concerned with whether you can heal the sick, walk among dead souls and pronounce life. They do not care about grandness of speech but whether you can pray a prayer that tickles the very ear of God.

Too many singles are walking around concerned about miniscule and trivial matters such as the size of their sexual organs, the shape of their breasts, the condition of their savings account, and the fatness of their investment portfolio. When it is all sifted through God's idea of what matters, these things slip through the cracks. What is left standing and matters the most are the qualities mentioned in Philippians 4:8: "Finally, brethren, whatsoever things are true, whatsoever things are honest, whatsoever things are just, whatsoever things are pure, whatsoever things are lovely, whatsoever things are of good report; if there be any virtue, and if there be any praise, think on these things." (KJV) The answer to question # 2 lies in this passage of scripture. If you want to know what you could offer your potential helpmate, the qualities listed in Philippians 4:8 would be a great starting place. Imagine the richness of your relationship if the two of you offered to one another those things that were true, honest, just, pure, lovely, of good report, virtuous, and praiseworthy! How awesome your commitment level would be to one another if she depended on you for these things and in return showered you with the same.

The size of your wants and needs is a greater determinate of the type of soul mate with which you will end up in life. During your selection process, you have to differentiate between your wants and needs. You may want one thing but need something totally different. For example, I might DESIRE to satisfy my sweet craving daily with a bowl of cookie-dough ice cream smothered with chocolate syrup and whipped cream. But, I might NEED a salad instead. Likewise, I may really desire to date or marry a certain kind of woman. But, because of my work in the ministry and life-long goals, God will send me what I NEED. Are you willing to accept what God sends your way? Or, are you determined to satisfy your life with the things you desire instead?

When God is ready to move you in that direction, He will make himself clear. It will be as obvious as a ketchup stain on the collar of a white dress shirt. Who he sends your way may or may not fit every area of what you desire, but this person certainly will be exactly what you need. So in the end, does size really matter? The answer is, "Yes!" Size does matter when selecting a mate. However, it is not the size of your bank account, genitalia, or even a house that matters. Instead, your hands should be strong enough to hold your mate's heart; your heart should be tender enough to soothe your mate's mind; your mind should be sober enough to understand your mate's needs, and your feet should be large enough to take you where God leads.

Love Handles: What things do I have to offer my spouse? What am I expecting from him or her?

Chapter 11

No Time for Games and No Room for Mess

—〽—

Proverbs 2:11-15 — *"Discretion will protect you and understanding will guard you. Wisdom will saved you from the ways of wicked men, from men whose words are perverse, who leave the straight paths to walk in dark ways, who delight in doing wrong and rejoice in the perverseness of evil, whose paths are crooked and who are devious in their ways."*

The Bible warns of those who manipulate the lives and hearts of others for personal or evil gain. In the book of Proverbs, we find sound instruction for handling people in our lives that enjoy playing games and occupying our lives with mess. Proverbs 2:10-11 states, *"When wisdom enters into thine heart and knowledge is pleasant unto thy soul; discretion shall preserve thee, understanding shall keep thee."* In other words, when we are dealing with the affairs of life, we are encouraged to use WISDOM. My God, how awesome this scripture is! Think about it; wisdom produces discretion. And discretion, in turn, will preserve and keep you. We need to be fully aware of what we are allowing our souls to experience during our dating season. Singles must enter relationships with both eyes open. This does not mean that we are to be overly suspicious. But, we are encouraged to be reasonably cautious, remain focused, and be aware of the direction the relationship is taking.

During a recent family Christmas get together, I enjoyed watching my son and nephews open their gifts. I marveled at how they all bypassed the clothes, shoes, and gloves for the much more stimulating motorized cars, computer games, and action figures. Their enticement with games reminded me of my younger days as a child. Most of my favorite games (*stickball, king of the hill, and marbles*) did not require much equipment, just a group of neighborhood kids looking for fun. Throwing water balloons off the roof of my house or climbing the trees on our block were the highlights of our day. As goofy as that may sound to some of my sisters in Christ, climbing trees and jumping off roof tops were actually helping to shape my perception of friendships and relationships.

Incidentally, the girls in the neighborhood were learning how to interact with their peer group when they dressed up their dolls, played a game of kickball, or sketched out a game of hopscotch. These activities taught us how to cooperate, work as a team, and develop character. But, as I matured, I abandoned most of my childhood games. Frankly, games became less exciting and seemed quite immature for me to engage any longer. After all, nothing can be goofier than a bunch of thirty-year olds playing a game of "Catch a girl, kiss a girl!" Right? Well, what may seem odd is actually quite common among Singles today. Unfortunately, people are still playing games!

Facilitating Singles Ministry meetings at my local church, I listen to the endless cries and frustrations of singles who are tired of the social games people are playing. Even as I reflected on my days of *dating gone wild*, I could not help but empathize with them. It was obvious that countless numbers of brothers and sisters were suffering from broken hearts and developing negative attitudes toward relationships even as they continue to play games with their lives.

Singles, realize that after playing years of adult *Hide N' Seek, Catch a Girl-Kiss a Girl, and Doctor,* it takes several years of healing before you can trust anyone with your heart again. Moreover, when the man or woman of your dreams does come along, you are not ready because wounds have still not healed from the last disastrous relationship. Listen to what Paul says about game playing and immature Christians. *"When I was a child, I talked like a child, I thought like a child, I reasoned like a child. When I became a man, I put childish ways behind me."* (I Corinthians 13:11) In today's vernacular, Paul is saying, *"Back in the day, I acted like a child and played a lot of games with folk and ran games on folk. But, now that I have grown in my relationship with Christ and my knowledge of Him, I've given up my sinful ways, quit playing games, and decided to grow up!"* Wherever you are, stop right now and yell, "Quit playing games!"

I am convinced that the main reason so many Singles are unable to fully grasp the privilege of being whole in their walk with God is that too many are caught up in playing games or being played. Unfortunately, some remain in this perpetual state of childhood. However, the Bible offers examples and consequences for this state of mind. For example, we find that Jonah played games with the Almighty, and we see where it landed him! Furthermore, the Bible tells us of how Saul *played the fool* and Gomer *played the harlot.* Also, Joseph's brothers thought they had run the ultimate game on him. However, they did not factor in God's sovereignty.

Now, because games often lead to traps, let us talk about traps. You start off playing games only to look up one day and find yourself neck first in the grips of a trap designed especially for you. While advising a caller on her financial woes, Dave Ramsey alluded to the reason that people remain in traps. He intimated that people find that they cannot get out of the trap of debt for holding on too tightly to the cheese. Of course, there are other traps in which we find ourselves occasionally. One of the most common among singles is the trap of Long Engagements. This is a trap mainly because it does not take ten years to determine if you have found the one! For instance, one of my single friends dated a man for over two years, yet every time the subject of marriage was mentioned, he dodged any discussion. For two years, the two of them were stringing one another along only to dissolve their relationship in the end. One wanted just an intimate friendship and the other a romantic covenant. Now in her forties, the woman is panicking that her time may have run completely out and that her happiness as a bride may never be realized.

Listed below are a few scenarios that I have encountered during rap sessions with Singles who were trapped in the games of deceitful relationships. See if you can relate:

Female A dated Male B for a year and seven months before finding out he was actually still married; he had been separated for five years. Despite the temporary separation, Male B had no intentions of divorcing his wife. Since it was apparent he was not going to quit his game, Female A made the decision to quit and get out of the game rather than continue being played!

Female D dated Male C just long enough to pay off several of her credit cards, co-sign for a car, and purchase a number of department store items. Sadly, he was not the only one she was scheming—there were several other men (oops...I mean male friends) in her life. Since she was obviously more skilled at the game of deception than he, his decision was apparent—cut his loses and quit the game!

Male E and Female F were inseparable in public and the envy of family and friends. Neither was interested in pursuing a marital relationship, however. In fact, both were quite comfortable with their arrangement of cohabitation. In the privacy of their one bedroom apartment they despised each another greatly. Rather than let go of the false image they had created for family and friends, they chose to go on torturing one another emotionally and relationally by remaining together!

Female G and Male H have been sexually involved with one another for over seven months. They have an open relationship and have maintained a sexual relationship with other partners as well. Male H refers to Female G, however, as his MAIN thing. Ironically, Female G is flattered to hear she is his main love interest. Quit playing games people!

Nevertheless, I Peter 2:1 states, "*Laying aside all (game playing) malice, deceit, hypocrisy, envy, and all evil speaking, as newborn babes, desire the sincere milk of the Word, that you may grow.*" Singles, I challenge you to put down your game pieces and make a difference for God's kingdom. There is power and wisdom awaiting you in serving Him. Set your affections upon God first and allow him to guide you in your pursuit of a holy, healthy, and wholesome dating relationship that is exclusive and drama free!

Love Handles: To which of the scenarios before mentioned can you mostly relate?

Chapter 12

No more test drives!

I Corinthians 6:18 – *Flee from sexual immorality. All other sins a man commits are outside his body, but he who sins sexually sins against his own body.*

When I ventured out in search of my first new car, I visited practically every car lot in Memphis. I visited car lots with American made cars and foreign made vehicles as well. Each time I arrived on the lot, an eager car salesman approached me with an offer to test drive one of his slick models. Some of the vehicles I test drove were obviously out of my league, budget wise. Others appealed to my monthly budget but didn't impress me at all with their exterior or overall driving features. Nevertheless, whether the car was too expensive or within my budget, exquisite or shabby looking, I test drove each one. Most of the cars were new but already had nearly one hundred miles already registered. My trips around the block added an additional 5 miles. When I found the car of my dreams, I made an offer that was well below the price the dealership was asking. I offered less because the car had already been driven several miles, yet it was still considered by the dealer to be a new car.

Promiscuous lovers are like the test driver in the story above. They visit car lot after car lot, church after church, club after club in search of various models/women/men. If the driver likes the way she looks on the outside, he requests a test drive to make sure the engine is working and interior is clean. All the while, he has no intention of buying the model. And, if the naked truth were revealed, he probably could not afford the car anyway. Test drivers delight, nonetheless, in taking the car around the block as many times as the dealer will allow without a commitment to buy. Oddly enough, even if the car is not appealing on the outside, it is not uncommon to find the driver taking it for a test drive to see what is under the hood. Ladies and fellow brothers, at some point, you have to stop and think about the number of miles you have accumulated and realize that your value decreases with each test drive. The more miles, the less the final offer is. As good as you may look on the exterior, the interior tells it all. Even the engine is experiencing the wear and tear of drivers who could care less about the future owner.

Actually, the whole game of test-driving is a matter of irresponsibility. The Word of God encourages men and women in I Thessalonians 4:3-4 with these words, "For this is the will of God, even your sanctification that ye should abstain from fornication: That every one should know how to possess his vessel in sanctification and honor (KJV). Essentially, what the writer is urging believers to do is acknowledge God's will for their lives – to remain holy by abstaining from sexual activity not sanctioned by God. Additionally, the writer makes the point that every one of us should be able to possess our vessels with respect and responsibility. For men, our vessels are our penises and for women their vaginas. In verse 7 of this same chapter, the scripture states that "God has not called us to be impure, but to live a holy life." God designed our bodies for His glory, not for the world's pleasure.

If you are a man, you are to keep your vessels with responsibility. Contrary to popular belief, you are not God's gift to every woman. Keep it to yourself until such a time that God honors you with a wife, and, to her and her only do you share your gift. It is a life or death matter. Stop today! The Bible tragically records, "Neither let us commit fornication, as some of them committed, and fell in one day three and twenty thousand" (KJV – I Corinthians 10:8). When 23,000 men die as a result of the world's largest orgy, it is apparent that God was displeased with a bunch of players! The scripture is referring to the book of Numbers chapter 25. The men of Israel decided to indulge in a mass sexual orgy with the heathen women in Shittim. While they were engaging in these affairs, they even bowed to their gods. While the men were being pleasured by these women, they lost their sense of spiritual relationship and obligation to the one true God almighty.

Is this not how it usually goes with us as well? God is usually the last person on our minds during romantic interludes. If we are not careful, we will find ourselves doing and saying nearly anything. These acts of passion were out of the will of God – thus considered sinful. As with all sin, consequences follow. But, often times, we have no control over the type of consequence issued. This particular time, God instructed Moses to kill these promiscuous men and hang their heads in the sun for the rest of Israel to see.

There had to have been about a 1,000 men beheaded because later when God allows a plague to wipe out 23,000 more folk, Paul records the total lost as 24,000. That is a lot of people! But, many more men and women are falling and dying daily as the pandemic of promiscuous lifestyles continues even today.

The message is clear as to how God expects us to govern our bodies. From the pre-teen curious about sex to the college student experiencing his or her first instance of freedom, God says, "Flee fornication." He does not say linger around and play with it for a while; he does not say lay in bed with it and quote scriptures rebuking it all the while; he does not say think on it day and night and entertain it via the internet; he says FLEE! Flee means to literally run for your life. In other words, move with such gusto as if your life depended on it.

During one of our Singles' Ministry meetings, my pastor used the firecrackers example to describe how we treat fornication. Symbolically speaking, every time we engage in petting and foreplay, we are lighting the fuse to a host of connected firecrackers. What we often do is stop the action when one person speaks up and says, "We need to stop before this goes further." The fuse is put out temporarily, only to be lit again next Friday on the second date. This ignition and diffusion action continues until the wick becomes so short that lighting it again leads to all out sexual intercourse. Now, the whole thing blows up in both your faces. And, the consequences for your actions may include disease, pregnancy, guilt, and/or a continuous memory of a time you were out of the will of God.

The past is odd, in that, it shows up every now and again at the doorsteps of our mind, knocking loudly. And, upon opening the door, we are greeted with a, "Hi! Remember me? I am the stupid thing you did years ago, and I just wanted to remind you of the event." I hate this about the past, but I love the mercy and forgiveness that is given through Christ. Without Christ, I would not be able to function properly. His blood declares me clean, forgiven, and free! Then God casts the act into the sea of forgetfulness. He does not remind me of it; it is the enemy that does that. But, whenever the enemy comes knocking at the door of my memories, I ask Christ to answer it for me. How do I do this?

I simply pray, "Jesus, I know my past and I know that you know what I have done. Because you have forgiven me and declared me right before God, I am no longer bound by the guilt of the past. Help me, today, Lord not to repeat the same acts that brought you shame before."

Today, my fellow brother or sister in Christ, the test drives must CEASE!

Love Handles: Pray this prayer with me… Lord God Almighty, God who convicts and converts but also forgives and loves; I confess that I have sinned. Each time I engaged in sexual activities with another, I brought shame to you. I have sinned and fallen short of your glory and grace. But, today I ask you to have mercy upon my soul. Please forgive me and cleanse me from all unrighteousness. Please strengthen me from this point forward to walk in integrity and holiness. Help me to be strong in the face of temptation. Condition my mind to live a life of abstinence. Allow my spirit to find satisfaction in you Lord. And, teach me to bring my flesh under submission daily. I love you with my whole mind, heart, soul, and strength. I give you the glory for all you have done and continue to do for me. In the name of Jesus the Christ, AMEN.

Chapter 13

The ABC's of Abstinence: A recipe for remaining pure

—ɱ—

Colossians 3:5 — *Put to death, therefore, whatever belongs to your earthly nature: sexual immorality, impurity, lust, evil desires and greed, which is idolatry.*

The best thing my wife offered me was a challenge to my biggest struggle – she made me wait! I do not know of many in my circle of peers that can say that they married their spouse without even tasting her lips first. Most singles I know believed in the motto that you have to test the waters before you decide to buy the ship. Or, in the South we say it like this: Before you buy the car, you better take it on a test drive around the block. This mentality has messed up the lives of so many saints that I feel compelled to challenge it in this chapter. I want to pass on some sage advice on how to live an abstinent lifestyle. The scripture says in Colossians 3:5 to put to death (or kill) whatever is earthly in nature, such as sexually sinful acts, lusts, and impure thoughts to name a few. All during my years as a single's pastor, I encountered countless individuals who were beating themselves up over sexual acts of the past. "How can I stop?" they would ask. I never had the perfect answer for this question. But, I was able to share with them what was working for me.

At the age of 27, I decided enough was enough. No longer would my spirit man allow me to get away with declaring God's Word but living according to the world's standards. I was preaching to the youth to keep their pants up and skirt tails down but was leaving Bible study on Wednesday preparing for sex on Saturday night with my girlfriend. And, in my mind, since she was a girlfriend, it was okay. At least it was in a committed relationship, right? Wrong! So, against all worldly standards and much to the chagrin and some- times anger of girlfriends to come, I declared abstinence. Like anything, it was hard to accomplish at first, especially the starting cold turkey. But, you cannot treat sex like a water hose and turn it off gradually. If you are going to do it, you have to shut the valve off immediately, without hesitation.

For the next eleven years, I had some good days and some challenging days, but I held on to my commitment to God. I was determined to let this be my testimony of God's grace, mercy, and deliverance all in one! One relationship ended after only a month of dating. She had formerly been involved with an abusive guy and was relieved to be in a relationship with a man who valued her and taught her so much about herself and her relationship with God. But, after being told repeatedly that I had no plans of being involved sexually, I was given the famous Dear John letter and kicked to the curve. This one hurt...

Not only did this woman cast me aside because she could not as she said, "...continue at the pace we are going without having sex," but she also made the choice to revisit her rela- tionship with her abusive ex-boyfriend. In other words, it felt like she was saying to me, "Since you refuse to meet my sexual needs, I will go back to something not good for me, just to have my sexual needs met." Mannnnnn! That hurt. I almost slipped up and gave up the fight at this point. I started questioning if this thing was worth it and where I would end up in life. I was tired of being the butt of all of the jokes — of exploding or imploding from the build up of unreleased passion. I wanted relief and would have turned away from my mission, if it were not for the grace of God.

On that same day, I recall taking a long walk in the mall, hurting, when God reminded me that it was all going to be worth it in the end. What was so awesome was that He made it plain that my reward would not just be received when I got to heaven but in this lifetime, I would see the glory of the testimony of holding on to His promises. While walking in the mall that day, God led me to a jewelry store where I had once purchased a watch. It was there that I cast my eyes upon one of the most impressive gold wedding bands that I had ever seen. It was a simple diamond cut band with several crosses embellished around the body of the ring. It was the last one in the store; I purchased it without hesitation!

"When is the big day," the clerk asked. "I have no idea, but it is coming," I replied. Can you imagine the look on the clerk's face? God instructed me from that point forward to wear the ring on my right hand for at least two reasons.

1. To remind me of God's promise to me and my promise to Him. Every time, I looked at my hand, I knew of the goal I had in mind.
2. To provide a constant testimony of my vow of abstinence to those who inquired. Daily, without fail, someone would see my ring and comment on its style. That opened the door of witnessing for me. I would share what I was doing and give them the testimony of how long I had held true to it. I had opportunities to talk to countless people and share the love of God with them.

Now listen, I applaud you and praise God for his sustaining power over you if you are reading this and are still maintaining your virginity. How awesome a place you are in life to have such a precious gift still contained in your soul. You are special and the gift you possess is not only unique but also priceless. You have what I could never reclaim. However, if you have tasted the fruit of pre-marital sex already, do not lose hope. All is not lost. You can begin today renewing the life of holiness you were intended to walk. I know how you think God sees you. And, you would be right in your assessment were it not for the blood of Christ that covers you and me. He sees us as righteous because of Him who died for our sins. Yet this does not give us a license to continue to wallow in the sin state of uncontrollable lust.

Now let us be real with one another. As easy as it sounds, it is not easy to lead a lifestyle of abstinence! For many of us, sex has been placed in a high priority on our list of daily accomplishments. But, the unfortunate component for singles is that God has not granted us a license to indulge in this act. If sex were a car, singles would have no reason even sitting behind the wheel. Singles do not have a license to drive. "But, technically," you may say, "Minister Jones, I am not driving the car; I am just getting a feel for the road and how the car handles. We are not about to go anywhere yet."

Let me say this really loud – I am not stupid! If you keep sitting behind the wheel, twisting it, turning it, and pretending to be driving, pretty soon you will get the gumption to crank it up. It will not be long after that you will be driving on the road as an inexperienced driver with nothing more than practice stimulation (Oops, I meant SIMULATION). And, no one without a license to drive needs to be on the road headed anywhere; the best thing for you is to get out of the car and admire it from afar until the day that God bestows His license upon you. You ask, "How can I walk away from such a tempting set of wheels?" I am delighted that you asked this question. Below, I have furnished a few strategies that should aid you in discovering the lifestyle of abstinence that God desires for you.

THE ABC's of ABSTINENCE

A — Accountability Partner: Pray that God reveals to you two accountability partners. These are friends or relatives that you do not mind getting into your business. They know your strengths and weaknesses. They are aware of your vow to abstain from sexual relations. They are folks who do not mind getting in your face and asking you the tough questions. They check on you regularly to make certain you are still on the track. You will hate them at first but love them in the end.

Name at least three individuals that would make excellent accountability partners—folks that would have permission to get into your business for the purpose of making certain you maintain a walk of holiness.

1. _____
2. _____
3. _____

B — Be honest with your dating partner: Let them know up front your decision to hold off on intimate contact. This is fair to them in the beginning so they can make a decision to remain with you or flee. If they remain, remind them that you need them to be just as accountable and not attempt to sway you away from your goal.

C — Celebrate small steps: It can be a trip to the doughnut shop or a simple turning of a cartwheel. Either way, enjoy your accomplishments and praise God for his keeping power each week you are successful. We celebrated during our Single's Ministry meeting one Friday night when we found that half of our members had maintained their abstinence for several months. Even the members who boasted of weeks of abstinence joined in our celebration.

D — Distinguish between love and lust: Too often, people get wrapped up in the emotions and lust of the relationship while neglecting to develop the love. Understand that lust and emotions are present instantly. But, it is the love that one has for another that will take time to mature. The type of love I am alluding to is not EROS. That is the erotic love that drives the lust and all of the passion that you are not ready for in a non-marital relationship. I am speaking of AGAPE love, an unconditional love that looks past faults and wrongs. Despite the fact that this person is not the most ideal mate you would have imagined, you are still able to love him or her. When you think about it, you may not be the most ideal mate either. So, just as you are imperfect, you learn to love those who are imperfect. When you invest more AGAPE time than EROS time, you decrease the likelihood that you will end up on the receiving end of a lustful relationship gone wrong.

E — Elicit the support of prayer partners: Tell others of your plan for abstinence and ask them to pray with you and for you in the beginning. Their prayers will strengthen you, especially as you embark upon the first couple of months. The prayers of the righteous people in your life will avail much. Ask family, friends, and even co-workers to pray for you and for your choices. You will find that not only will God's will become clearer but also that your choices will become much wiser. You will be a happier more fulfilled person without the confusion of being sexually tied to another.

F — Filter seductive images/sexual thoughts: A few images of seduction on the big screen or a sexy romance novel detailing the sexual affairs of two characters is all that is necessary to kick your hormones in overdrive. Stimulation can arrive in a number of packages. Even our own thoughts can sometimes stray into the realm of ecstasy if we are not sober and vigilant about maintaining holy thoughts. I do not mean that we have to walk around twenty-four hours a day with nothing but scriptures and worship on our minds. But, the more we preoccupy ourselves with thoughts that glorify God, the less room remains for the enemy to infuse wicked images. Even married couples must be intentional about discarding ungodly thoughts from our minds.

G — Guard your eyes: Protect your eyes because they are the portals of your soul. What we see, we develop in our minds. Sometimes, we overdevelop the images we see, especially men. Men are prone to do a double take when spotting a beautiful woman from across the room. Just that image alone, if left untamed, can lead to a host of thoughts.

H — Handle your vessel with honor: When the Bible speaks of a person's vessel, it is alluding to a person's body, especially their genitalia. Possessing one's genitals with honor essentially means remaining pure and reserving sexual pleasures for his or her spouse. Married couples must abide by this rule as well; it is a good idea to put into practice what is required in the marriage bed.

I — Identify your weaknesses: The enemy has a resume on us and knows our weaknesses. Therefore, we must be aware of what could take us down. Everyone is not the same; we each have our own idiosyncrasies. For example, it would be hard for me to resist chocolate brownies with pecans and ice cream or about a half dozen glazed doughnuts even though I know they would destroy me if I consumed them daily. But, placing a box of fig newtons or a slice of coconut cake before me would have little effect. Why? The latter does not tempt me to indulge. When you know what tempts you, you avoid exposure to it as much as possible.

J — Join a singles Ministry or group that supports your beliefs: These persons will make great accountability partners as you strive to maintain a lifestyle of abstinence. I headed a group for more than eight years. These members were the people that encouraged my walk and held me accountable to the ministry God was birthing in me. They kept me focused on the purpose of abstaining for God's glory. If there is not one in your town, organize your own with just a few friends. Before long, it may grow to impact thousands.

K — Kill the flesh: This is easier said than done. Killing the flesh involves quickening the spirit man within you. The more you feed your flesh, the stronger it becomes. The more you feed your spirit man, the stronger he becomes. It makes sense, if you are going to profess God as your Father, then you feed the man that matters the most. The flesh should be fed pot-roast not porn. But, when we allow our flesh to be fed porn our spirit becomes corrupt and weak. You must kill the flesh by feeding your spirit with prayer time, devotional time, along with praise and worship time. Build him up to be more victorious than defeated.

L — Learn to avoid compromising situations: If you find yourself at the end of a date in the bedroom with the lights completely off and the music of Luther Vandross blaring in the background, there is a pretty good chance that something is about to occur that you will end up regretting in the morning. There are some factors that increase the likelihood that a sexual encounter will take place. Learn to identify them and avoid them at all costs!

M — Move forward with your life: So you messed up! Okay, repent and get over it. Instead of dwelling on the mistakes of the past, even if it was last night, it is a good idea to get up from your bed of guilt and move forward. God needs you at one hundred percent. So, trust that he has forgiven you and make a serious commitment to NOT indulge anymore. It is time to move forward.

N — Never expect more than you are willing to give: Do not assume that giving in to sexual pleasures with the person you are dating will cause him or her to become more committed to you. It does not work that way. True commitment works well in marriages when both persons are working at it. In a dating relationship, it often fails because of one person's partial commitment to the partnership. The ultimate commitment is not the guarantee that I will go out with you next weekend. The ultimate commitment is, "I do take you as my wife." That is the type of commitment that is not given just because you slept with me last week.

O — Obey God: He is our father and requires our obedience. Obedience is basic to any parent-child relationship. Even earthly parents expect this of their children. We obey God by adhering to what His Word expects of us. God wants to protect his children from the harm caused by sex outside of his will. So, he instructs us to wait until we have married our soul-mate before we share what is precious. To share with several people what God has ordained as exclusive disrespects Him and the person for whom it was ultimately intended. Practice daily obedience.

P — Pray continuously for strength, especially during down periods: There were periods in my life as a single that sexual tension was not an issue. But, during those times when I was at my weakest, I had to really seek God for strength. There were times when I had just finished preaching or teaching God's Word and worship had been at its highest. However, in my winding down period when all was quiet and settled, I found myself being tempted at all points and from all directions. Never let a day go by without talking to God and praying for strength to make it through another hour.

Q — Query: There is nothing wrong with asking questions for clarification. If you do not understand something, the best thing to do is ask questions about it. Sex is complicated when it takes place out of the will of God. So, a good starting place for answers to your questions is the Word of God. The Word gives explicit advice on the purpose of abstaining and the blessings of waiting until sex is ordained of God. Before you query your favorite tabloid, magazine, or journal, I would definitely seek what God has to say first.

R — Recognize the moves of the enemy: His ways are deceitful and damaging. His whole mission is to seek us out, steal what he can from us, kill everything that resembles God, and ultimately destroy us. This is precisely what sex out of the will of God does for our soul. It is damaging. So, deceptively, he introduces people in our lives who do not agree with our mission of abstinence. He places those things and people in our paths that tempt us the most and beckons us to entertain them. Recognize his ploy and avoid him altogether. Flee full speed ahead if you must.

S — Surround yourself with positive people and rid yourself of negative folk: Positive people enhance our lives. They think, walk, talk, give, and live differently from negative thinking folk. The vibes and connection you feel with positive people exceeds the drag and drain of hanging with negative people.

T — Try alternative dating strategies: For some, group dates are the way to go. Group dates take the focus off of intimacy and places the night's events in the category of friends having a nice outing. Still others have found that dating in an open arena during the daytime without the stimulation of dark lights and soothing music is ideal. Skating rinks, bowling alleys, putt-putt golf centers, and botanic parks are a few of the non-threatening locations for alternative dates.

U — Understand that abstinence is a lifestyle, not an event: You have to keep this in your mind and comprehend the process fully. Just going through the motions one time is not enough. Daily, you have to recommit to the challenge of successfully abstaining from sexual promiscuity. It is similar to a diet done right. When I consider a diet as an event, I am likely to eat healthy today but binge tomorrow. However, if I consider a diet as a lifestyle change, I become sensitive to what I am allowing my system to digest daily. I make a conscious effort to do right daily because I UNDERSTAND it is a process, not an event.

V — Volunteer your time serving God and meeting the needs of mankind: God has positioned singles in a unique place in life. You have the freedom to serve without reservations. Often times before I can even think of volunteering my time, I have to consider my wife's needs, my child's needs, and our household needs. By the time I consider all of these responsibilities; the opportunity for service has usually passed or seems undoable. Volunteer your time at nursing homes, prison ministries, homeless shelters, children's hospitals, schools, or even community agencies.

W — Walk away from unhealthy relationships: You do not need anything unhealthy in your life. Would you ever think of digesting slices of raw chicken sandwiched between two slices of molded bread and a couple of rotten tomatoes for breakfast every morning? Then why would you continually allow unhealthy people to remain in your life? I promise you that you will feel like a new person once you walk away from unhealthy influences. Try it!

X — eXamine your walk daily: It is important that you keep your walk holy before man and God. You cannot afford to keep slipping up if you are trying to move forward. Know where you stand and definitely be aware of where you are going. Your goal is to maintain a lifestyle of abstinence until such a time that God allows you to unite in matrimony with your soul mate.

Y — Yearn for a closer fellowship with Christ: Seek God while he may be found. Develop an intimacy with Christ that surpasses any earthly relationship you have ever had. Get so close to God that you begin to take on his image.

Feed off his Word daily and learn of Him. There is so much more to be revealed.

Z — Zip up your pants or skirt and leave the zipper in locked position: Your days of dropping your clothing for every tickle of the flesh are gone! Your clothes are your covering. They are only to be removed for two reasons – to wash or to change into another article of clothes.

Extra Love Handles: Keep track with the number of days, weeks, and months that you remain abstinent and celebrate your accomplishments regularly.

Section 3

Walking On Water
And Other Miracles

—𝔪—

It Must Be Love
By E. Marcel Jones

There's something that's keeping us together
And, like a sticky piece of tape, I can't get rid of it
Just when I think I've broken free of you
I find that it is still attached to me and you

There's this thing binding us together
And, it's kind of like a rubber band
Stretching just enough to allow some movement
But, not enough to break us apart

There's this substance holding us together
And, it's a lot like glue
Forming a seal so tight
That no one would ever be able to tell
where there was once a fracture

There's this force pulling us together
And, I swear it feels like the same thing
That held Christ to the cross
No, not the nails; but LOVE

And, it's more durable than iron
So much stronger than steel
Tougher than leather
Mighty enough to withstand any kind of weather

It pulls, binds, keeps, and holds
Our souls so tightly together
So tight your God becomes my God
Your people become my people

And we celebrate each other
Because we are one!

Chapter 14

How to Be At Your Best
On Your *WORST* Day

—⁓—

Job 14:1 — *Man born of a woman is of a few days and full of trouble.*

How has your week gone so far? Has it been pleasant for the most part? Have you had any major obstacles you have had to overcome? Have any of your days been considered bad days? Have you ever had one of those days, Singles, when everything that could go wrong went wrong or when the poop of life seemed to be using you for target practice? You know, the days that the car would not start. Your hair or attire refused to cooperate. Your money was at an all time low. Your employer decided to lay you off. Your grade report for the semester put you on academic probation. The list could go on and on and on! Yet, Job 14:1 remarks that we really do not have many days on earth. And, most of these days are going to be full of trouble. If this is true, then odds are that if you are ready for this chapter, you too have had a bad day at some point in your life. And, if you have not yet experienced a bad day, just keep living.

I recall a couple of bad days I have had in my life. When I was a child, I remember having a headache for three days that rendered me motionless. The pain prohibited me from raising my head from the pillow. Those were some bad days. I recall the ninth grade assembly program at my junior high school when I fell from the third row of the bleachers in front of my peers. That was a bad day! I can even reflect on days when I waited on my next paycheck with less than ten dollars in the bank. Those were bad days! Yet, through it all, none of my worst days even partially compare to the last day of Jesus' life on earth.

Do you remember the day when Christ was crucified on the cross for our sins? To begin with, this day was not the best day for pleasant weather. The clouds and winds were unpredictable. It became suddenly dark; the earth shook violently. There was likely an overcast as God positioned the clouds and heavens so that they hid his eyes partially from the brutality his son had to endure. This day started out weather-wise to be a bad time for a crucifixion. In the second place, it was not a good day for Jesus in court. He lost his case but watched a guilty man be set free. It was not a good day for family reunions as he watched his mother endure the pain of seeing her son crucified. It was a bad day emotionally. Jesus at some point on the cross felt abandoned by his Father and betrayed by his friends. He endured ridicule and public humiliation. Yet, on Jesus' worst day, He was at his very best!

How can we be at our best on our worst days? I believe the answer to this question can be found in the final words that Christ spoke while on the cross. In these seven sayings, there are seven principles to put in practice on your worst day.

Luke 23:34 records the first saying - Then Jesus said, "Father, forgive them, for they know not what they do".
To be at your best on your worst day, you have to maintain a forgiving heart. In this life, one fact is certain, folk will do you wrong. However, one more thing is for certain, and that is that you and I will wrong someone as well. You have either wronged someone with your tongue, your hands, your lips, or your mood trips. In fact, a young lady confided in me her struggle with forgiving a former friend who had turned on her and who now had become her enemy. My reply to her was, "You must forgive others because God forgave you." We must all forgive because we have been forgiven. Consequently, on your worst day, do not forget to ask God to have mercy on others. For sometimes, people really do not know the extent of what they are doing.

2ⁿᵈ saying - He said to the thief on the cross, "Truly, I say to you, today you will be with me in paradise." (Luke 23:43)
From Jesus' words to the thief on the cross, we extract another example of how to be at our best on the worst of days. Understand that this world is not the end of life as we believe it! As good as it gets at times for some of us, I hate to halt your tour of Oz, Dorothy, but this world is not paradise. Conversely, as BAD as it gets for the rest of us, the good news is that it is not HELL either. Furthermore, what is even better news is that all of our bad days have expiration dates. The older saints used to put it this way, "I'm so glad, trouble don't last always." The scriptures remind us that "weeping may endure for a night, but joy will wake us up in the morning." Whether it is morning on earth or morning in heaven, trouble cannot last always. Therefore, on our worst days, remember that true paradise and eternal glory awaits those of us who have trusted our lives in Christ. Whether we are in a hurry to get to heaven or not, it is just good to know that this life is not the end of the story.

3ʳᵈ saying - Jesus saw his own mother, and the disciple standing near whom he loved, he said to his mother, "Woman, behold your son". Then he said to the disciple, "Behold your mother!" And from that hour, he took his mother into his family. (John 19:26-27)

Out of respect for the emotional burden his mother was experiencing, Jesus took time out during his own suffering to delegate his mother's care and provision to his most trusted disciple, John. On your worst day, never forget to acknowledge and show care and concern for your family. Do not take it out on the family because you are having it rough in life. In other words, do not bring home your bad day and take it out on those in your household. One of my friends has a doormat that reads *LEAVE YOUR MESS HERE*. Indeed, leave the stress of work and messy attitude outside. As challenging as it gets at times to love your family members, they really are all we have. Husbands, wives, moms, dads, brothers, sisters, nieces, nephews, and in-laws are all a part of who we are. So, even on your worst day, do not forget you have a family who is concerned about you as well.

4ᵗʰ saying - Around the ninth hour, Jesus shouted in a loud voice, saying "Eli Eli lama sabachthani?" which is, "My God, my God, why have you forsaken me?" Matthew 27:46 and Mark 15:34)

Jesus again takes the opportunity during his suffering to talk to God. And, just as honest and sincere as he was when he prayed to God for forgiveness of others, he is again honest with God about how he feels. He asks God why he has forsaken him at a time when he needed him the most. At some point during your worst day, it is always good to take some time to talk to God. Situations may not change instantly, but God has a way of conditioning us to hold on a little while longer. When you find yourself nailed to the cross for the good of humanity, it is prayer that conditions you to endure the suffering. When it looks like everyone has forsaken you (family members, friends, and now even the God who promised never to leave you nor forsake you), you must hold on to your faith. God is not slack on his promise. He has never left us. In fact, because you and I are still holding on during our worst day is evidence that God was here all the time. So, since he is here, do not forget to map out a few moments to talk to Him on your worst day.

5th saying - Jesus said, "I thirst". (John 19:28)

5th saying - Jesus said, "I thirst". (John 19:28)
    Who would have ever thought that the Living Water would one day become thirsty! This passage teaches us that Jesus was as much divine as He was human. The time on the cross is now likely between twelve and three o'clock in the afternoon. Jesus, in a parched tone, utters the words, "*I Thirst.*" Fatigue had set in at this point; the heaviness of grief lay upon his heart. The heat of the day and excessive loss of blood was now causing this deep natural thirst. Warren Wiersbe said, "Jesus thirsted that we might never thirst." Jesus became thirsty and endured the cross so that we would always have living water to quench our spiritual thirst. He is the wellspring that never runs dry. Just as Jesus paid close attention to his physical needs, we too must not only nourish our souls with spiritual food but also feed our physical bodies the basic food and water it needs. The stress that is brought on by a bad day can take its toll on our bodies. Accordingly, be wise to listen to the needs of your physical man.

6th saying - Jesus said, "It is finished". (John 19:30)

6th saying - Jesus said, "It is finished". (John 19:30)
    When Jesus said it is finished, he was alluding to that fact that all of our sins would now be forgiven and that the guilt that should have been reserved for us to carry was now taken on by Him. Indeed, it is a victorious cry that what he was sent to accomplish was carried out to completion. This part of the work of salvation was now done. But, we know

that God was still not through. Jesus would die, be buried, be resurrected on the third day, and then ascend to heaven to take his position at the right hand of the father. Yet, that is still not the end of Christ's work. Notice that this is the second to last saying, not the last word! Whatever God begins in your life he will also complete. No matter what the day looks like now, there may still be work for you to do.

On your worst day, understand that God is still not through with you. If this is the worse, then imagine what is in store on the other side tomorrow. God is saying to you right now that if you think things look bad, just give him three days, and he will turn the situation around in your favor. On your worst day, do not get wrapped up in whether this is the end or not. Instead, focus on what God is doing in your life at this very moment. You will miss the magic of his mighty power if you focus on how bad the situation is.

This may be the end of one thing that is about to usher you into a new beginning. The divorce may be the doorway to the new beginning that God has planned just for you. The death may very well be the staircase to the beginning of a new path that God is directing you to take. The breakup, as bad as it hurts right now, is likely the window of opportunity that God has been preparing and anointing you for all along. God is not through with you yet.

The 7ᵗʰ saying - Jesus said, speaking in a loud voice, "Father, into your hands I commit my spirit". **(Luke 23:46)**
You better know at the end of the day who is the master of your soul. It is ludicrous to spend your entire life gaining worldly possessions only to lose your soul because you failed to gain salvation through Jesus Christ. William Ernest Henley, in his final words before being executed, penned these words in the poem *INVICTUS.*

Out of the night that covers me,
Black as the Pit from pole to pole,
I thank whatever gods may be
For my unconquerable soul.

In the fell clutch of circumstance
I have not winced nor cried aloud.
Under the bludgeoning of chance
My head is bloody, but unbowed.

Beyond this place of wrath and tears
Looms but the Horror of the shade,
And, yet the menace of the years
Finds, and shall find, me unafraid.

It matters not how strait the gate,
How charged with punishments the scroll,
I am the master of my fate;
I am the captain of my soul.

Contrary to the words of this poem, we are not the captain of our souls. God is at the helm of this ship. I can barely navigate through the perils of life, so I learned a while ago to turn over complete control of my soul to the one who set this world in motion, God almighty himself. And, surely, when we leave this earth, we have no clue how to navigate our souls to heaven. Once again, we need the divine hand of God to usher us into his presence. Thus, at the close of even your worst day, just before you lay down with the expectation of getting up again in this life, you better pause to make certain your soul is anchored in the salvation of Jesus Christ. Even on my best day, I would not leave my soul's future to chance. Make certain that your soul rests in the bosom of God. Your worst day may or may not be your last day, but it helps to know that whether it ends today or tomorrow, God is indeed the captain of your soul!

Singles, now that you know how to be at your best on your worst day, make certain you have mercy on others, recognize that this life is not all there is; take the time to care for family; take the time out to pray; take care of your body; remember that God is not through with you yet; and make certain that your spirit is secure in the hands of God.

Love Handles: Describe your worst day. Which of the seven principles did you apply?

Chapter 15

God is Bigger Than Your Past

—ɷ—

Micah 7:8-9 – Do not gloat over me, my enemy! Though I have fallen, I will rise. Though I sit in darkness, the LORD will be my light. Because I have sinned against him, I will bear the LORD's wrath, until he pleads my case and establishes my right. He will bring me out into the light; I will see his righteousness.

A commercial featuring an elderly woman who had fallen to the floor and could not get up aired years ago. As serious as this commercial was, it became a humorous phrase to use whenever a person suffered a slip or fall. For me, the phrase rang loudly on the day I slipped from the third row of bleachers at my junior high school. As I excitedly made my way to the stage to receive a cash award from our school's sponsor, I slipped and therein began a series of tumbles. When I finally arrived on the floor, there was not a dry eye in the place. No, these tears were not the result of sympathy but from hysterical amusement at my fall. The entire gym erupted in laughter and began finger pointing. For a seventh grader, it was the end of life as I knew it. Surprisingly, though the memory lingers even today, I have recovered and survived to share it. In fact, I have grown stronger as a result of this event.

There are occasions in every Christian's life, especially single Christians, when a fall is inevitable. We are not perfect and even the most studious and devout Christians fall. But, just as I lived to tell of a fall from my past, many of you reading this chapter need to know that God is bigger than your past – no matter how blemished, shocking, disgusting, embarrassing, or unfortunate it may be. You may have fallen, but you can get up. How do you know this Minister Jones? Because, I have fallen a few times in my life, but each time I got up with the saving grace of God. I will likely slip at least a few more times, but as long as God provides me with "Getup ability," I will rise to tell of his glory and mercy. Getup ability is the action God takes when he restores us to right fellowship and puts us back on the path to living for Him.

When it comes to falling and getting up, falling down is not difficult. Quite frankly, falling is an easier feat than getting up. Mental falls occur when thoughts that do not glorify God enter our soul, and we entertain them. Spiritual falls occur when God plainly tells us to go here, do this, speak that, yet we sit still, remain inactive, and become silent. In other words, falling occurs whenever we fail to carry out the will of God; when we sin, we fall. When we rebel against God, we fall. The sin of disobedience is often at the core of our falls. Moments of disobedience are like riptides. I like to call these moments *riptides of disobedience*. Riptides are those undercurrents that carry you further and further out to sea if you are not careful. I recall my first encounter with the strong forces of riptides while swimming one summer. I had not mastered the art of swimming, floating, or treading. Yet, I kept testing myself to see how far I could wander into the depth of ocean waters. Before long, I found myself up to the neck in water. With panic written all over my face, I tried desperately to fight against the undercurrents that were pulling my body further out with each swelling wave. By the grace of God, I was able to gradually make my way back to shallow areas.

Much like riptides in water, disobedience takes us past the point of return and attempts to destroy us. This is why is critical to avoid such acts of rebellion. Obedience is the answer to fewer falls. Further investigation of the scriptures gives us more insight into state of fallen Singles. From the scripture in Micah, we learn the following principles:

Never gloat over someone's fall, especially one of God's children. Using the words of F.B. Meyer, my pastor, Gary Faulkner, reminded our congregation one Sunday to never gloat over a person's sin. He preached that we should never judge a person who has fallen because we never know how many demons have been assigned to that person nor how many times the person has been successful at resisting them. What may look to us like an individual who willingly indulged in adultery or fornication may, in fact, be the result of Satan's lifelong attack on one of God's most influential leaders. Those who claim they never face temptations of any sort need to check whose side they are own in this Christian walk. Any true believer is going to be tempted by the enemy and occasionally attacked or challenged with rebellion towards God. But, with each attack of the enemy affords the opportunity for victory in Christ. And, as the song rings in my old country church in Trezevant, Tennessee, "...Each victory will help you, some other to win. Fight manfully onward, dark passions subdue, He's willing to aid you, and He will carry you through." If you should happen to fall in your resisting, know that God provides the opportunity for you to repent, get up, and begin again.

Though a man fall, he can get up! It is a simple equation. You and I need to get up more times than we fall down! If we fall seven times, then we need to get up eight times. If we slip up twelve times, then we need to find our way back to our feet thirteen times. God desires to use singles that are not defeated and down trodden. Christ told the dead young damsel in Mark 5:41-42, "Little girl, get up!" He announced to the paralytic man who sat by the poolside in John 5:8, "Rise, take up thy bed, and walk." What would have seemed cruel, making a dead girl get up or announcing to a paralyzed man to get up and walk was actually God's way of moving his gospel forward through delivered folk. If you have fallen, you can get up! You have to get up! Why? Because, God is bigger than your past falls and failures.

Falling is inevitable so it is not a question of IF I will fall, but a matter of WHEN. This is important to know so that when we fall, we do not beat ourselves into uselessness. Nothing is as defeated as wallowing in the cesspool of guilt and shame, especially when God is standing with outstretched arms to help us get back on our feet.

Never underestimate the forgiving nature of God. Minister Jones is not able to forgive you for your past. Indeed, at times, it is hard for me to forgive myself. But, God can forgive and is willing to cleanse you from all unrighteousness. I John 1:9 states, "If we confess our sins, He is faithful and just to forgive us of our sins and cleanse us from all unrighteousness." That is great news considering I have messed up so many times before. To know that when I repent of my sins and confess my sincere and deep remorse for my sins, God is standing faithfully each time ready to forgive and cleanse me. As bad as it may seem to me, my fall is worse in His sight! However, because I have a blood relationship with his Son, he sees me as cleansed.

In fact, the only reason I can get up after falling from God's grace is because of my faith in Christ Jesus. The privilege of approaching a thrice holy God is all because of Jesus. The blessings I enjoy are because of my relationship with Christ, my Savior. The mercies I wake up with each morning are due to my steadfast faith in the one who died that I might have life and have life more abundantly. When God raised Christ from the dead, he guaranteed me "getup ability" too. Therefore, Jesus' resurrection does at least two things for our ability to get up after a fall. Let us examine them.

His resurrection gives us a <u>reason</u> to get up—He did not die for us to stay down. I John 2:1-2 – *"My dear children, I write this to you so that you will not sin. But if anybody does sin, we have one who speaks to the Father in our defense— Jesus Christ, the Righteous One. He is the atoning sacrifice for our sins, and not only for ours but also for the sins of the whole world."*

Secondly, His resurrection gives us the <u>strength</u> to get up. According to Philipians 4:13, *"I can do all things through Christ which strengtheneth me." (KJV)* And, Ephesians 6:10 states *"Finally, my brethren, be strong in the Lord, and in the power of his might."* My ability to get up and regain strength rests in God's power. Based on this truth, my fall is only temporary and never permanent.

According to a survey reported in the *Discipleship Journal* (November/December 1992), readers ranked the following areas of greatest spiritual challenge:

1. Materialism
2. Pride
3. Self-centeredness
4. Laziness
5. Anger/Bitterness
6. Sexual Lust
7. Envy
8. Gluttony
9. Lying

The readers additionally noted that temptations tended to be more aggressive when they had neglected devotional time with God or were physically exhausted. The following suggestions were given for combating temptations: engaging in prayer time, utilizing personal study time, avoiding compromising situations, and developing accountability partners. Each of these suggestions is vital to your walk. Implement each of them daily and decrease the number of falls you are experiencing.

Love Handles: In which of the areas below do you fall most often? Have you given up hope of ever overcoming these areas?
___*Ungodly speech*
___*Sexual immorality*
___*Wrong motives*
___*Finances/stewardship*
___*Lack of devotional time/prayer time*
___*Disobedience to God's calling/voice*
___*Entertaining unholy thoughts*
___*Failing to spend time with family/children*

Chapter 16

Surviving a Katrina of the Heart—

—*w*—

II Corinthians 4:8-9 — *We are hard pressed on every side, but not crushed; perplexed, but not in despair; persecuted, but not abandoned; struck down, but not destroyed.*

This chapter is not about disastrous storms as much as it is about disasters of the heart. It is, in fact, a narrative regarding the tragedy of heartbreaks and breakups. It is a message to never-married Singles that you can survive a **Katrina** of the heart. It is a message to divorced singles that you can recoup from the bitter storm **WINDS** of separation and loneliness. It is a decree to single widows that God can and will wipe away the **FLOOD** of tears that the death of a soul mate created. Singles nationwide should have been able to sympathize and relate to the evacuees of Louisiana, Mississippi, and Alabama. And, anyone who has ever loved knows what it feels like to suffer a broken heart. Much like the after effects of a storm, a Katrina of the heart can render a person hopeless, helpless, hindered, and down right bitter! But, using the scripture above, I have come to offer hope to

Singles who never thought they would survive a Katrina of the heart.

First, understand that some of us have encountered so many Katrinas of the heart that we use the memory of these past hurts as milestones in our lives. Often times, we may find ourselves reliving these moments through reflective thoughts. *Ohhh, I remember my first love...." or "Man, let me tell you about this one girl I was crazy about...." or "I vowed I would never let myself love like that again, especially after...."* You know the stories—you have heard them, lived them, and lived to tell them! But, do not be quick to dismiss them. There are lessons we can all learn from Katrina so that we do not find ourselves inviting future devastation in our lives time and time again.

First, though a Katrina of the heart is often unpredictable it is always preceded by a series of warnings.

Hurricanes do not just show up in the United States unannounced. Usually, high winds, smaller clouds, and heavy rain precede the very eye of the storm. Likewise, a Katrina of the heart occurs after several warning signals have sounded and obvious danger signs have surfaced. Once the Holy Spirit has sounded his initial warning, there is but one response—FLEE! Heed the voice of the Lord and get out while you can. FLEE! In fact, the sooner you get out of the way of its destructive course, the better your chances of coming out alive. Have you ever gotten so involved with a deadbeat that you feel you have invested too much time to let him or her go despite the unhealthy connection you both have? The longer you stay in that situation the dimmer the voice of the Holy Spirit becomes because you have ignored his plea so many times. I have one word for you—FLEE!

Secondly, you cannot wait until the last minute to be prepared for the devastation of a Katrina of the heart. For several reasons, many remained in New Orleans despite the warnings. Some felt they could treat it like all of the other mediocre storms that they had experienced. Few of them could fathom the devastation Katrina would cause with her powerful winds and horrific floods. After the storm had subsided, the flooding waters appeared. It was learned that more people had perished as a result of the flooding water than the ravaging winds. Just as those who remained in New Orleans felt the worst was over when the storm had passed, many of us feel we can treat every broken heart the same. NOT! A Katrina of the heart will fool you into thinking it is really not that bad. Please know that there are some Katrina storms designed to take you out of here. That is precisely why God's grace had to be written all over your life. The last Katrina event should have taken you out of here. But, God be glorified – You are still here!

Preparing for a Katrina of the heart involves your staying in touch with God before, during, and even well after the breakup. Psalm 1:2 states, *"But his delight is in the law of the Lord; and on his law he meditates day and night."* You need to understand that your relationship with God is critical to your survival. And, the best way to nurture a relationship with God is by spending time in His presence. Preparation also involves prioritizing. Every now and then it is good to prioritize the stuff as well as the people in your life. What is valuable? Who is important? Very likely, you will lose some possessions after Katrina is through with you; things will not be the same. That is why it is crucial for you to prioritize and take notice of what things are needed in your life to make it more fulfilling. You will find that what you thought was important, really is not; what you thought was healthy really was not. In fact, the mantra you should adopt is, *"If it is not growing, it is dead weight!"*

Finally, remember no matter how rough the winds of adversity blow or how high the flood of tears rise, continue to hold on to Faith and Purpose.

I love the words of the song that state, "When you get to the end of your rope, reach up and tie a knot!" There are two knots you should hold on to tightly in the aftermath of a Katrina. First, hold on to your **faith in God**. Whatever happens or whoever leaves you, do not let fear overpower your faith. Exodus 14:13 states, "*...Do not be afraid. Stand firm and you will see the deliverance the LORD will bring you today...*" Be steadfast in your faith and exercise it daily. Your faith builds muscle, and muscle in turn aids in stamina and resilience. You will find yourself not only surviving major storms but also rebounding from the effects of the storm when you hold true to your faith in God.

Just as important, hold on to **God's purpose for your life**. Do not allow envy to overshadow God's individual purpose for your life. "*I will praise thee; for I am fearfully and wonderfully made: marvelous are thy works; and that my soul knoweth right well.*"—Psalm 139:14 KJV. Raise your head and realize that God has purposed you to experience more than this temporary setback. There is so much more in store for your life. Although a Katrina of the heart can reveal what you value, it cannot define who you are. The Katrina experience I survived left me *better* not bitter. Oh yeah, I was bitter at first; I was more upset with myself for not heeding the signals, but after I regrouped, regained, and renewed my faith, I realized that God was once again protecting me from greater disaster. And, if it meant his allowing me to feel the pain of brokenness and separation, I understood that He was keeping me from something worse than a broken heart. As II Corinthians 4:8-10 confirms, we might be troubled on every side, but somehow the Holy Spirit makes certain we are not distressed. Some of us might find ourselves perplexed, but the power of Christ will not allow us to remain in despair.

Still, Singles, you may find yourself persecuted, but God reminds you that you are never forsaken or forgotten. And, even if that Katrina of the Heart leaves you feeling cast down, keep in mind that at least you are not destroyed! Try using some eagle instinct the next time you encounter a Katrina of the Heart. Eagles are some of the most fascinating creatures to study with regard to surviving storms. I have read that when a storm begins to blow, an eagle will fly into the starter winds of the storm and allow the wind's currents to propel it upwards so much so that it literally rises above the storm. There, above harms way, the eagle rides out the duration of the storm. It literally uses the storm to escape from the storm! Isaiah 40:31 reminds us, *"But they that wait upon the Lord shall renew their strength; they shall mount up with wings as eagles; they shall run, and not be weary; and they shall walk and not faint."* *(KJV)* Take it from Isaiah, take it from me, and take it from the evacuees of Hurricane Katrina; you can survive and God will provide!

Love Handles: Have there been moments in your life when you felt you would never recover from a breakup, divorce, or death of a significant other? What lessons of deliverance can you extract from this chapter to begin your recovery process?

Chapter 17

For Anyone Who Has Ever Had To Start Over

—ɷ—

Ruth 1:3-5 — *Now Elimelech, Naomi's husband, died, and she was left with her two sons. They married Moabite women, one named Orpah and the other Ruth. After they had lived there about ten years, both Mahlon and Kilion also died, and Naomi was left without her two sons and her husband.*

Perhaps one of the most difficult experiences in life is the days after a breakup or death of a spouse. It is at this point that a person finds himself or herself having to star over. After losing the person one once loved, everything begins afresh and anew. For singles who dated their girlfriend or boyfriend for months and even years, starting over can be a dangerous and trying period. Likewise, for the widow, who after years of growing together as one, this period can be quite frightening? Even for divorced singles, who often find a weight lifted from their shoulders after enduring the hardships of a marriage gone awry, the period of starting over can be very intimidating. In Ruth chapter 1, we encounter three women, Naomi, Orpah, and Ruth. Naomi, the mother-in-law has been without her husband for years. While Orpah and Ruth, her daughter-in-laws, have recently lost their husbands of ten years. All three are now widows; all three are at a point of starting over again.

I thought of three brothers in my life that had all experienced loss of some kind in their relationships. One friend lost his wife of eight years to cancer. In the same month, another friend was served divorced papers by his third wife. And, at the close of the year, another dear friend confided in me that because of his promiscuous behavior, he had fathered a child with a woman that was not his girlfriend. Of course, upon discovering his infidelity, his girlfriend decided their relationship needed to end. As a result, three men; three losses; three lives faced with starting over again. Through their eyes, I realized that at any given point all of us, married or not, can experience loss. And, after all, each of us can experience starting over at the most unexpected times of life. I guess this is another reason why married people need this chapter as much as singles. At any given point, we too may have to start over.

Though full of trepidation, singles faced with times of beginning again must be careful to avoid common mistakes. One of the most common mistakes experienced is attempting to fill the void left gaping wide by a death, divorce, or breakup. Referencing the passage of scriptures in Ruth, there are some principles to follow if you ever find yourself having to start over.

Principle #1 – Do not allow your hormones and emotions to guide your next steps.

This point is critical as you begin again. Hormones are raging inside you, and just as likely your emotions are running rampant. But, as much as they may beat against your flesh, DO NOT allow them to dictate the direction of your steps. Allowing hormones or emotions to control you, could result in your making poor choices in future relationships or lead to a downward spiral of fruitless and lustful failed relationships. Yes, hormones and emotions are part of the soul. They are what make us even more individualized. But, the reality of hormones and emotions is that they are surface stimulants. Thus, although they exist and at times become intense, they cannot be relied on to make logical and sound decisions regarding life situations. This is the time to rely upon God's divine intervention and the voice of his Holy Spirit. Proverbs 16:9 states, "In his heart a man plans his course, but the LORD determines his steps." Allow God to do one of the many things he does so well – lead and direct your steps.

Principle #2 – Take several days and even months to reflect on what went well as well as what things did not work in your past relationship.

Be honest with yourself as you record these items in a journal. What role did you play in making things work? What mistakes were the results of your doing? Are you looking forward to another relationship? If so, what do you expect out of it? What aspects of your own personality do you plan to keep? What aspects would you change? These are critical questions to answer prior to making your next step, assuming you plan to make a next step. You do not want to remain stationary and unproductive. Therefore, a do not allow the tragedy of separation to cause your life to hinder your growth as a person. You have to keep living. It happened; it was unfortunate; things have and will change. Yet, you must continue on for your sake, the ministry's sake, your gift's sake, your family's sake, and, most importantly, for God's sake!

Principle #3 – Cling to those who are near and dear.

Notice that as Orpah made the decision to return to the familiar, Ruth decided to cling to Naomi at the risk of experiencing the unfamiliar. Ruth was young and I am certain the men were swarming about to be the next in line. Although she knew little about what was ahead, she knew enough to put her trust completely in her mother –in-law. Wherever Naomi went, Ruth would go. Wherever Naomi rested her head, Ruth would follow. Naomi's people would become Ruth's people. And, even more importantly, Naomi's God would become Ruth's God. What an astounding impact to have on another person's life when your lifestyle and walk cause them to follow you in this manner. Nonetheless, it is important to cling to genuine people. The men I mentioned at the beginning of this chapter were literally attacked by droves of women who had learned of their single status. Some wanted to comfort; others wanted to be considered the replacement. These men had to protect themselves from unwanted solicitation by clinging to family members and friends who genuinely had their best interest at heart. Neither would be ready to even consider another relationship until they had healed. During their healing process, it was important that they cling to individuals whom they could trust.

Principle #4 – Look to Christ as your Kinsman-redeemer.

If anyone can restore that which was lost, it is Jesus Christ. Allow his favor to fall upon you. Your responsibility is to maintain a walk of integrity. God will do the rest. Notice how Ruth gleaned daily in Boaz's field. From day one, her reputation preceded her. Townspeople, including Boaz, had heard of her selfless efforts to remain by her mother-in-law's side. She had a walk of integrity and honor. This was probably more attractive to Boaz than even her looks. The first day he saw her, he asked, "Whose woman is that?" She looked so put together that she had to be taken already. God has a way of preserving his children. You will experience similar situations as you begin again. People will wonder who you are and be attracted to your disposition and the way in which you carry yourself. Your walk says it all.

Principle #5 – Expect your latter days to be greater than your former.

As beautiful as your life may have been or as rotten as it could have been prior to your loss, understand that the days following will be sweeter. Not only does restoration promise to renew your life but also the plan of God assures us that days ahead will be even brighter. Because God's plans are bigger than our finite minds, we cannot begin to understand why the loss was necessary. Remember that Ruth had to lose her husband in order to line up with God's plan to further usher in the lineage of Christ. Through Ruth and Boaz's union, Obed was born. Obed was the father of Jesse, who we know to be the father of David. David was to be the future king of Israel. And, so on and so on.

You really do not have a clue as to why God allows the divorce, death, or breakup. But, what you can know is that even these events could be part of God's plan to position you to be where he needs you to carry out His ultimate plan. Therefore, expect that your latter will be greater than your former.

Love Handles: Have you ever suffered the loss of someone and had to begin again? Which of these principles were most critical to successful living?

Chapter 18

On My Way to Oz,
I Found Myself!

—⟋⟋⟍—

Luke 15:16-17 – *He longed to fill his stomach with*
the pods that the pigs were eating, but no one gave
him anything. When he came to his senses, he said,
'How many of my father's hired men have food to
spare, and here I am starving to death!'

In the 15th chapter of the Gospel according to Luke, we find
one of the most beautiful evidences of God's ability to find
lost objects. He opens in verses 1-7 discussing the parable of
the lost sheep, continues in verses 8-10 with the parable of
the lost coin, and concludes in verses 11-32 with the parable
of the lost son. In the parable of the lost sheep, a party is
thrown when one of the ninety-nine is found. Likewise, in
the parable of the lost coin, a woman and her friends rejoice
over finding one of ten pieces of silver. Even in the parable
of the lost son, a celebration like never before occurs when
one of two sons returns home after being lost in the world.

The one passage that particularly captured my attention
and motivated me to write this chapter can be found in verse
17 – "And, when he came to himself…" I love it! I can relate

to this young man as I am certain many of you can as well. I recall a time in my life when I too had reached an all time low, only to have God open my eyes wide enough for me to realize that this was not where I needed to be. Have you ever been there in life, when everyone else is looking at you in amazement at how far you had fallen, but you could not see it for yourself? It took God and his divine revelation to help you "come to yourself." The New International Version (NIV) of this passage says – "And, when he came to his senses..." Thank God for his Grace!

The parable of the lost son reminds me of one of my all time favorite movies — The Wizard of Oz. For years I have always watched the movie for the music and overall enjoyable characters. Having matured, I grew to appreciate the many messages about life portrayed throughout the movie. There are as many themes as there are characters. There are, however, six main characters that remind me of my years as a single person. The story of the Oz is complex yet simple. Simply put, it tells of a girl named Dorothy preoccupied in her mind with getting out of Kansas and living in a better place — somewhere over the rainbow. After being struck unconscious during a tornado storm, she dreams that she has been catapulted into the Land of Oz where she and her dog, Toto, meet a host of characters that are also in search of what they too are lacking. The rest of the movie is devoted to Dorothy, a Scarecrow, a tin woodman, and a cowardly lion heading off to meet the Wizard of Oz who supposedly is able to grant their needs.

What is interesting is that the main characters resemble the lives of people we may have encountered in life. Dorothy, for example, reminds me of a misguided person with the power to change things at his or her very feet. Yet, Dorothy type people continue to frantically search for a way home. Ironically, before the Tornado, it was this very home from which she wanted to escape. However, now that she finds herself in a strange environment, she longs for the familiar again. Incidentally, the scarecrow she encounters is the perfect picture of an incompetent individual. Here stands an ineffective man charged with one responsibility – keeping the crows away from the corn. And, that simple task, he fails at every time. Also, the tin woodman is the picture of an individual going nowhere. He stands motionless, rusted from years of immobility. Ironically, an oil can sits by his side the entire time. Tin woodman type persons have at their very fingertips what it takes to be successful, yet they remain paralyzed and motionless. Finally, the cowardly lion was the picture of disappointment. Everyone expects the King of the Jungle to be courageous. However, cowardly lion type people have lost their roar. Without a roar, issues are never resolved and the person falls prey to everyone and every situation. Whenever a person loses his or her roar he or she also loses his anointing, power, and even position.

Thus, the lost son in Luke 15 embodies all four characteristics. Like Dorothy, he was more enamored with the world and what it had to offer than with his own home. And, just like Dorothy, when he discovered that the world was more than he could handle, he longed for home! Much like the scarecrow, the lost son needed to retrieve his brain. No longer was he thinking logically or spiritually. We find him about to dine on the hogs' dinner. It was apparent that he failed to use common sense when governing his financial affairs. Both the lost son and the tin woodsman have much in common as well. They both appear to have lost their passion for life. Both have reached a point of non-productivity. The resources are available, just not in reach. And, just like the cowardly lion, the lost son had lost power, prestige, and position. His ring was gone; clothes were torn; and he reeked of odor from a pig's stall. But, it was the boy's Father not the Wizard that restored him back into his rightful relationship.

Maybe, you too have found your life in a whirlwind. You have landed in an Oz of your own world. And, suddenly, you find that your life has taken on the characteristics of one of these characters. You have agonized over what seems like an endless and hopeless cycle of being stuck in non-productivity and powerlessness. The Good News is that God, our father, is able to restore you. But, the restoration begins with you! You must first realize your present state of being and be honest with yourself. You are not where you should be or even where you used to be. You have slipped to an all time low. Moreover, in realizing where you are, remember where you must go. The lost son in the parable of the prodigal son, at the point of dining with the hogs realized his deplorable state in life. But, as quickly as he realized his state, he remembered his father's house. There, he would find food, clothing, and employment as a hired hand. Anything his father would spare would be better than what he had in hand at the present time.

Just as the lost son, you must return to your Father —- your heavenly father. Therein realizing your state, remembering your father's house, and returning to his arms, you must also repent of your wrongs. Confess to the father all you have strayed away from and all that you have indulged in freely. This is not the time to dress it up. Tell it like it is and call it what it is. Then, step back and watch God renew your life, remove the stench of sin, and restore you once again. On your way to Oz, stop by and see the Father!

Love Handles: What character in the story of Wizard of Oz has your life at some point closely resembled?

Chapter 19

Peer Pressure: Keeping the Crowd Happy

—ɯ—

Mark 15:15 — *Wanting to satisfy the crowd, Pilate released Barabbas to them. He had Jesus flogged, and handed him over to be crucified.*

No matter how much we age in the coming years or how much older we will be next year, we will always have peers. Peers are persons in our age range. And, where there are peers, there is always the possibility that peer pressure will exist. Contrary to popular belief, peer pressure does not just go away after the adolescent years; it continues to hang around well into our twenties, thirties, and even fifties. Peer pressure has been said to be the tipping point for many sins committed. Most of the time, we are already on the edge of doing right versus doing wrong. All that is needed is a gust of wind to push us over the edge in one direction. And, the wind that blows is often the influence of peers. It only takes a little encouragement from single friends to sway us in one direction or the other. As you read the passage above, it should have been interesting to learn that Pilate also suffered from peer pressure. At first, it seems the passage is really about Jesus' being on trial before Pilate. But, in fact, it is actually Pilate who is on trial before God. Pilate's true character is revealed as he stands in the very presence of the Son of God.

For Pilate, the decision he faced was not one of whether Jesus was innocent or guilty; he knew Christ was innocent. His decision became one of satisfying the crowd versus doing what was right in God's sight. He suffered from peer pressure! For us, our character is on trial each time we deny our faith before mankind. When we fail to do what is right in God's sight and follow the urging of the crowd or world, we fall victim to peer pressure. Moreover, when Singles live a lifestyle that is contrary to God's plan but in accordance with the world's terms, they reject the standards of their faith. Every one of us stands in this place at some time, face to face with God in a place of decision. Like Pilate, we teeter in our souls whether to do what is right or to do what pleases our peers. Too often, in our attempts to appease people in our lives, we neglect what is right. And, just as Pilate, we find ourselves in a situation where our character is tested.

In the beginning of Mark chapter 15, the Jewish leaders brought Jesus to Pilate for judgment. Pilate, a Roman governor, was part of the regime that had stripped the Jews of their rights to inflict any type of capital punishment. Therefore, in order for Jesus to be condemned to death, he had to be sentenced by a Roman leader. If the Jewish leaders could get Jesus executed on a cross, they believed he would be cursed from God by dying on a tree. In fact, their whole motive was to convince the followers of Christ that he was cursed, not blessed, by God.

In addition, if Jesus were merely charged with blasphemy, it would not matter much to a Roman leader. Roman leaders did not practice the Jewish religion. Subsequently, the Jewish leaders fabricated three other charges and accused Jesus of tax evasion, treason, and terrorism. He was accused of encouraging the populace not to pay their taxes to Rome. This was an obvious false accusation. Furthermore, he was accused of claiming to be a King, specifically the king of the Jews. This was another false accusation because actually he was and remains THE KING. Finally, he was accused of causing riots all over the countryside. How people reacted to his miracles and teachings was not his fault. Thus, this was another trumped up false charge.

When you look closely at Pilate's dilemma, you can see the tension he must have encountered. For this small time Roman leader, a little position, a little power, and a lot of prestige could be easily threatened. The same crowd that gathered in John 19:12 were the same individuals that threatened to report Pilate if he did not turn Jesus over to be crucified. This is a critical piece to consider as we examine Pilate's choice. Because he was already on shaky ground in his administration, Pilate could have been in danger of losing his power, prestige, and position, had it been reported to Caesar that a riot was occurring. Therefore, Pilate compromised what he knew to be right to save what was never guaranteed. A lesson to take from Pilate is that God rewards those who do right and follow after righteousness. God does not reward those who make others happy at the expense of compromising what is right.

Romans 12:1-2 urges us "*...by the mercies of Christ that you present your bodies a living sacrifice, holy and acceptable unto God which is your reasonable act of worship. And, be not conformed to this world, but be ye transformed by the renewing of your mind.* Singles, I admonish you not to be conformed and refuse to compromise! Before you panic about losing your power, prestige, or your little position, stop and check your actions to make certain they are righteous and not routine. **Righteousness** sets a standard for others to follow, but routine-ness keeps folks around you happy! In Pilate's case, he was too preoccupied with what others would think of him if he did not go along with their demands. Whether it is a friend or a foe, you cannot worry about what people will think about you when you decide to do what is right. As for me, I have decided at the age of forty-one to follow what is right and not what is popular! I am tired of trying to satisfy the crowd. Can I get a witness?

James Crook said, "The man who wants to lead the orchestra must turn his back on the **crowd**." The reality of serving God is that everybody will not be happy with you all the time. So, rather than allowing the music to suffer, you must turn your back to the crowd and conduct the orchestra in front of you. Stop marching to the beat of other folks' rhythms; boogie to the beat of the tune that God has placed in you.

As we look at life through the lenses of today's scripture, I have extracted a few nuggets for us to hold onto:

1. You cannot trust the crowd because people are fickle. One day you may find them with you; the next day, these same people will stand in opposition to your agenda.
2. You cannot trust your position because it is temporary. The reality is that even kings die. There is no position that is forever or always guaranteed. In other words, you can be here today but gone tomorrow. I have witnessed supervisors replaced by floor employees in a matter of minutes. Singles, listen carefully to me; do not put your faith in your position.
3. You cannot rely on your prestige because it is too unpredictable. You may be at the top this afternoon but find yourself flat on your back later in the evening. When I watched the last NBA Draft, I was amazed at the number of players that were expected to go in the first round being picked up in later rounds. Prestige does not always assure success.

4. You cannot trust your power because it is on loan. Whisper in your own ear these words – *All power belongs to God*! Since all power belongs to God, what little power you and I think that we possess is really on loan to us. Therefore, before we embark on some venture in our own power, we need to realize that our success is contingent upon God's strength, not ours.

I hope this chapter blessed the reader who was about to make a decision based on what was best for the crowd. God is saying to you to consider what you know is right and not focus on what fickle folk in the crowd think. Be determined to follow what is right and not what makes the crowd happy. As once quoted, "It is not enough to have a dream unless I am willing to pursue it. It is not enough to know what is right unless I am strong enough to do it. It is not enough to join the crowd, to be acknowledged and accepted. I must be true to my ideals, even if I am excluded and rejected. It is not enough to learn the truth unless I also learn to live it. It is not enough to reach for love unless I care enough to give it."

Love Handles: How often do your peers influence your decisions in life?

Chapter 20

Damaged but Delivered

—〰—

Daniel 3:25 — He answered and said, Lo, I see four
men loose, walking in the midst of the fire, and they
have no hurt; and the form of the fourth is like the
Son of God. (KJV)

I would like to take you to a heated moment and extract
some life principles for you to use when you find yourself
in a precarious situation. These are some principles to apply
when you find yourself in a situation that is the result of your
obedience not your disobedience to God.

I deem that some of you believe life becomes a series
of opportunities and situations where we have the chance
to choose to do the <u>right</u> thing and honor God or <u>compro-</u>
<u>mise</u> our standards and faith system. The ultimate goal for
many is to find ourselves making wise choices more often
than compromising. In Daniel 3:16-19 Shadrach, Meshach,
and Abednego answered the king. They said, "King
Nebuchadnezzar, we know that we did the right thing. You
may throw us into the very hot fire. But the God to whom we
give honor can rescue us. He will rescue us from your power
if he wants to. But if he does not rescue us, we want you to
know that it does not make any difference. We will not give

honor to your gods. We will not give honor to the image that you have set up." Then Nebuchadnezzar was very angry with Shadrach, Meshach and Abednego. His face became red. He ordered his servants to make the hot fire seven times hotter.

Look closely at versus 23-25 — And Shadrach, Meshach and Abednego still tied up fell into the very hot fire. Then King Nebuchadnezzar was astonished and jumped up. He said to his officials, "Did we not tie up three men and throw them into the fire?" They answered the king, "You are right, our king." The king said, "But I see four men walking about in the fire. They are free and they have no injuries. The fourth one looks like a son of God."

I just wonder if some of you reading this book know what it feels like to stand up for something right only to be thrown into a heated situation with seemingly no way out. When the heat turns up in my home, you cannot get out alone. You are going to need a fourth man in your life. Some of you may find yourself in heated moments on your jobs. It is in matters such as these that you and I must rely on the delivering power of God. The people of Judah continually compromised their nation into a state of spiritual whoredom. Each day they slept with other gods. But, on the Sabbath they climbed into bed with the one true God.

I admonish you to listen carefully. You and I cannot entertain the world Monday through Saturday without regard for God and then awaken on Sunday and climb in bed with God. You would not allow it in your house, and God's standards will not allow it in His. Someone has to life up the standard of holiness. Hence, this is why I love this passage of scripture so much. Here are three Hebrew boys refusing to join the world's party, refusing to feast at the king's table, and refusing to bow to an idol. Shadrach, Meshach, and Abednego resisted the standards set by the world. They refused to be seduced into the spiritual mediocrity and the compromise that, ironically, had led their nation (Judah) into captivity initially. They remained true to God! On one occasion calling for all to bow down, the scripture records that Hananiah (Shadrach), Mishael (Meshach), and Azariah (Abednego) defied King Nebuchadnezzar's order and maintained their integrity. Nebuchadnezzar, upon hearing of their rebellion, ordered the boys to be thrown into a burning furnace. However, after they were thrown into the fire, something caught the king's eye.

It was not the fact that the men were walking around now unbound and free. Rather, it was the fact that instead of three men, there were now four men in the fire. The king remarked that the fourth man resembled some type of deity. It was the only way he could describe the God he had never encountered. He had compared Jesus the Christ to the false gods with whom he had come to trust. Contrary, the fourth man cannot be compared to any other. It is this fourth man that makes the difference when you and I are in the fire of trials and temptations. In truth, it might not be a bad idea to invite the fourth man into your next fire! The fourth man can determine whether a person is simply heated or completely burned. When Christ is present, He determines whether a person is comforted or all-consumed. With all that you have had to face in the last three years of your life, you really should have lost your mind by now. Yet, somehow the fourth man keeps stepping in and continually keeps you from being consumed. What an awesome God!

Everyday, just like Hananiah, Mishael, and Azariah, we too must face a world that sounds its instruments for us to bow down. As children of the most high God, we must also make decisions whether or not to compromise our faith. For this reason, my hope is that Singles are making wise choices to hold fast to the profession of their faith. I know that there are daily struggles you have to face when confronted by various distractions and influences of this world. Consequently, there are a few principles that I would like for every Single believer to hold onto whenever you find yourself on the verge of compromising your faith.

1ˢᵗ principle — **Never ever compromise your faith or your standards just because it seems like everyone else is bowing at the sound of the instruments**. This principle is especially important for all of us today. The Bible records that everyone bowed at the sound of the instrument; everyone except the three Hebrew boys who refused to compromise their faith and settle for less. Whether you are a teenager, married person, or single adult, the message is clear –never abandon your faith in the fire.

Teenagers, when the world suggests alternative lifestyles for you, embrace the type of lifestyle right for you. If you are married the enemy may attempt to whisper thoughts of infidelity in your ear, but, Married Christians, you do not need to bend or bow. In addition, single adults, when the world says spread your love around until you find the right one, **refuse to compromise**. Do not settle and do not compromise your faith or your standards for a quick thrill in the night. It is okay to say that you walk down a different road and march to a different beat.

2ⁿᵈ principle – **Every fiery trial you encounter is designed just for you, personally constructed with you in mind**. Understand that life's trials are uniquely designed to help us grow and mature spiritually. Every trial you and I encounter has been crafted especially for us. Our trials cater to us because they have been fitted according to our level of faith. Recall in Matthew 8:26 when Jesus remarked to his disciples on the troubled sea, "Why are ye fearful, O ye of little faith." Besides, our trials are designed according to the place to which God is working to get us. There are some places God is taking you that are not on God's agenda for me. This is why we do not go through the same tests at the same time. God fashions our trials with us in mind.

Tailor-made trials remind me of going suit shopping. A quality men's suit cannot be purchased from the rack without requiring some alteration. In other words, just because it says forty-two regular does not mean that it will fit me as it should. Most of the time, when I purchase a suit, I have to have material let out in the seat and waist. A cuff is added to the pant legs and the jacket usually requires some tapering for that broad shoulder look. I mean, if you are going to wear a quality suit, you may as well invest a few more dollars to make certain it looks like it was made for you! Indeed, God designs our trials much in the same way. Sure, at first it looks like your job loss is nothing uncommon. After all, there are countless numbers of folk who have been in similar situations. Losing a job looks like a common suit off the rack at first. But, God takes that common life occurrence and tailors it to your situation. The end result is a trial that only you could have survived. Some would have committed suicide; others may have reacted in a way that brought harm to co-workers. But, you...God gave you a peace that surpassed even your understanding.

Maybe your tailor-made trial is a rebellious child. For some, this situation would cause them to wash their hands of the child, leaving him or her to live a life without guidance and authority. Yet, it caused you to hold on even tighter and institute some periods of tough love. And, through it all, God allowed the fruits of longsuffering and patience to ripen daily in your life and in the life of your child. When you view fiery furnaces through the lens of the second principle, you realize that we have been strategically positioned to glorify God. It really is a royal set up. And, the quicker we understand this, the sooner we will be able to release our frustrations and move that much closer to deliverance.

3<u>rd</u> principle — At times, obeying God brings troubled times and seemingly impossible trials. Yet, these particular trials are for God's glory and our growth. You become the minority when you follow the unpopular routes in life. These three boys had no fear because they knew that obeying God in unpopular situations was designed to glorify God! Understand this, when God's glory is at stake, you can not lose! Examine these words from scripture: *Hebrews 13:5 – "I'll never leave you nor forsake you."* Psalms *34:19 – "Many are the afflictions of the righteous but the Lord shall deliver us out of them all."* These are basic promises of God that reassure us that our heated moments are not in vain. God gives us His promise to reassure us that we are not alone and *that "all things work together for the good of us who are called according to his purpose."* Romans 8:28. In fact, we know that nothing we experience for God's glory is in vain. All that we go through for God's sake is purposeful. Every problem, every situation, every circumstance has purpose. The purpose may be our spiritual maturity or simply that God be glorified. Sure, obeying God may introduce troubled times, but they are all for His Glory. So every morning, wake up with the expectation that, at any point, God can turn your situation completely around for his Glory and for your growth! I do not know what your situation is, but I do know that you are not alone. The Hebrew boys did not avoid the fire, but God did walk in the fire with them. God does not promise that life will be easy. But God does promise to be with us all the time.

> Isaiah 43:2— *"When you pass through the waters, I will be with you and when you pass through the rivers, they will not sweep over you, when you walk through the fire, you will not be burned; the flames will not set you ablaze! Why? For I am the LORD, your God, the Holy One of Israel, your Savior."*

Moreover, we cannot forget what God continually does for us. Countless times, he has rescued us from circumstances beyond our control. Think of the number of times, He has had to step into your life and correct wrongs. Each time you have needed him, he has been there. In fact, at times when you did not think you needed him, He made it his business to be there. I know there are times you cannot feel his presence or see evidence of his workmanship in your life. But, trust me, He is there. The belated James Moore, gospel recording artist, put it plainly in one of his greatest hits, "He was there all the time!" In every mishap, mess-up, mistake, and misfortune, God was there. Every moment of success, God was there. And, even now as you read the pages of this book, He is looking directly over your shoulder with you resting in the palm of his hand. He is there.

Incidentally, a father witnessed three little boys climbing a large oak tree in the neighborhood park. Thinking that they would hurt themselves by falling from the height they had climbed, he approached each of them and asked them to come down from the tree limbs by jumping one by one into his arms. Two of the boys without any hesitation or pause complied and leaped into the man's arms. The other child remained in the tree tops staring at the man below. A concerned mother who was also in the park asked the father why the third child refused to obey him. The father remarked that the first two boys obeyed him immediately because they were his very own children. They knew they could trust him to catch them and be there for their fall. However, he added, the third boy was not his child.

Singles, whether you are in a tree or in the fire, know that your heavenly father is concerned about your survival and desires to bring you to safety. He wants to deliver you and restore the damage caused to your soul. When you come out of this next fiery trial, you may be damaged but you will also be delivered!

Love Handles: Has God ever restored something that you once lost? Describe it...

Section 4

Right Style But Wrong Size

—⁓—

I Need A Wife
By E. Marcel Jones

I need someone who will intercede in my behalf
Without a hint from me that something's wrong
I need someone to read the map, while we navigate
Through unfamiliar territories in life

I need someone I can be responsible
for providing her every need
I need someone I can be myself with and
Not have to put on a full costume to have fun

I need someone who I can love God through
And someone who God, in turn, can love me through
I need someone who loves Jesus Christ
More than she loves the world

I need someone I can trust
And, someone who will come home
Every day after work to play

I need someone who doesn't mind sharing
The last piece of cake or half the can of soup
I need someone who knows the role of husband and wife
And, never allows the two identities to be confused

I need someone whose breast will nourish my children
Whose wisdom will educate their minds
Whose hands will discipline their wrongs
And, whose lifestyle will lead their paths

I need someone who is desires a lifetime with me
And, most definitely someone who needs me
Because, I need a wife just like you

Chapter 21

When Quit Looks Good

—ɯ—

Galatians 6:9 – *Let us not become weary in doing good, for at the proper time we will reap a harvest if we do not give up.*

There are occasions in our lives when situations become twisted, circumstances grow completely out of control, and events appear too chaotic. At these times, we really only have one of two paths to choose. One option is to keep moving forward and keep the hope of a brighter day alive in your spirit. The second option is to QUIT the course you are on and throw in the towel. In other words, when times get rough and clouds hang really low in our lives, we can either charge forward and fight or quit! What do you do when the option of quitting looks more appealing than holding on?

I must admit that quitting just seems a whole lot easier to accomplish, at times, than hanging in there. Think about it. The amount of strength required to hang on to something that is unproductive exceeds the simplicity of just letting go. Have you ever arrived at a place in your life when you have considered giving up on your search for a satisfying career? Or, maybe you have contemplated quitting a marriage gone sour. Could it be that school is too much of a load to carry at this point in your life? Or, possibly your health and finances are failing you at the same time. And, to make it worse, you now have begun to question whether your pursuit of spiritual excellence and holiness is really worth it. To put it plainly, you are not certain if you need to continue to serve God. Before you give up on God, however, I need you to finish reading this chapter. These words are for you.

God has made it clear to you on today that the reason your present situation is throwing you off balance is because you have become complacent with life. You have become accustomed to things working out in your favor. Your career, ministry, and even personal life have always flowed reasonably smooth. You have survived a great number of trials. In fact, you contribute your success so far to your good looks, wisdom, charm, finances, health, and motivation. In reality, however, it was God all along that has continually kept you. But, now, he has allowed you to become entwined in something that you cannot just charm your way through. He has you in a position that is not easily escapable. He has you at a place where you have to rely completely on Him to survive.

It is a scary place for you because of your past self-reliance, but it is also a necessary place for you. God is shaping you for a new position in life. You see the immediate situation in front of you, but God has a birds-eye view of what is ahead. Just like the news helicopter that flutters over a busy expressway, God sees the wrecks and exit roads up ahead. We see issues, but God sees solutions. God encourages us to not give up or pass out. There is deliverance and relief just around the corner. Stay in the RIGHT lane and keep moving forward.

Whenever you reach a point of giving up or quitting, remember these four spiritual truths to aid you through your journey. 2 Timothy 1:6-9 records, *For this reason, I remind you to fan into flame the gift of God, which is in you through the laying on of my hands. For God did not give us a spirit of timidity, but a spirit of power, of love and of self-disci-*

pline. So, do not be ashamed to testify about our Lord, or ashamed of me his prisoner. But, join with me in suffering for the gospel, by the power of God, who has saved us and called us to a holy life – not because of anything we have done but because of his own purpose and grace. This grace was given us in Christ Jesus before the beginning of time. Is God's word powerful or what?

The first principle to apply to a quitting spirit is to **stir up the gift that is in you.** You and I have been endowed with gifts from the beginning of our lives. Think about it. Before you were conceived, God was already thinking about your life and what trials, pitfalls, accomplishments, and victories you would encounter. That is simply awesome! I get excited over just the thought of being gifted with perseverance, strength, longsuffering, wisdom, and so much more. You and I are too gifted to quit. There is too much in us to fail now. The enemy, of course, would like nothing more than for us to lay aside our gifts and give up. But, the Word of God affirms that we have been blessed with gifts and empowered to overcome.

2 Timothy 2:1-3, 15 provides the foundation for our second principle. *You then, my son, be strong in the grace that is in Christ Jesus. And, the things you have heard me say in the presence of many witnesses entrust to reliable men who will also be qualified to teach others. Endure hardship with us like a good soldier of Christ Jesus. Do your best to present yourself to God as one approved, a workman who does not need to be ashamed and who correctly handles the word of truth.* When quit looks like the better option, **spend more time in God's Word.** It can be an hour or a couple of minutes out of the day. Regardless to the amount of time, you and I need to carve out times during the week to gather strength and knowledge from God's divine Word. Open up the Bible and explore what God has to say about your present lot in life. As a soldier knows the manual on

strategic warfare, God's soldiers need to know how to fight in the time of battle. Every situation in life is covered in the pages of God's Word. So, before resolving that you are the only person to ever go through what you are experiencing, read what God has to say to his good soldiers.

The third principle to apply is to **stand on God's promises.** Once you begin to delve into the Word of God, you will discover his promises. Unlike the promises of man, God's promises are always true. If God says that he would *never leave nor forsake us*, then you and I can count on *God's constant presence* in our lives. Even at times when we cannot feel him or see evidence of him, God is there. When the foundation beneath you becomes shaky and unstable, learn to stand on God's promises. *All Scripture is God-breathed and is useful for teaching, rebuking, correcting, and training in righteousness, so that a man of God may be thoroughly equipped for every good work* (2 Timothy 3:16-17). Simply put, the scriptures we read are all inspired of God. Therefore, his promises are true. As you stand on promises in God's Word, know that they provide the strength to hold onto during difficult times. Joseph stood on the promises of God and refused to quit. Take the lead from Joseph – You do not quit when you are in the pit. Your pit becomes the vehicle to move you into the palace and ultimately into position.

If the first three principles have not quite convinced you to hang on a little while longer, then possibly the last principle will. 2 Timothy 4:7-8 encourages us to **strive to keep Paul's charge**. As Paul wrote words of encouragement and instruction to a young preacher, Timothy, he penned perhaps one of him most commonly used statements. *I have fought the good fight, I have finished the race, I have kept the faith. Now there is in store for me the crown of righteousness, which the Lord, the righteous Judge, will award to me on that day and not only to me, but also to all who have longed for his appearing.* What an awesome resolution to continue the fight, finish what is begun in you, and to keep the faith. Fight, finish, and keep the faith. FIGHT, FINISH, and KEEP THE FAITH. This is not the time to give up. The reward of Galatians 6:9 is at your very doorstep. The promise is that if you faint not, you will be rewarded. Refuse to give into the situation. Instead, take the time to put up your fists and fast; roll up your spiritual sleeves and pray. Daily, make it your chore to work toward finishing what God has started. Strive daily to keep moving forward little by little. The goal is to not only see your deliverance but also keep your faith in God.

God longs to receive the glory in your struggle. But, he cannot get the glory nor can you receive the reward if you abort now. Two years ago, I planted some bulbs that never produced the flowers I had hoped. They did not sprout above the ground even an inch. So, after a few weeks, I gave up and decided to dig them all up and toss them in the trash. Apparently, I failed to dig them all up that spring. Three bulbs remained in the ground the entire year, even throughout the dead of winter. The following spring, the most beautiful flowers appeared. These flowers were the result of bulbs that had remained in the ground. Had I exercised some patience and allowed them to endure the heat of the summer, cold of the winter, and rains of springtime, I would have yielded a host of flowers instead of merely a few.

How does this relate to your situation? Stop quitting before God has had an opportunity to blossom you into the individual he shaping you to become. You are chosen for a task greater than you could ever imagine. So, before you throw in the towel or wave the surrender flag, realize you are not in this fight alone. God is not only in your corner but he is also the referee. So, no matter how rough things get, you will be victorious. Hang in there and look forward to what God has prepared for you. Each victory matures you and develops you into a strong believer.

<u>Don't Quit</u> – Anonymous

When things go wrong, as they sometimes will,
When the road you're trudging seems all uphill,
When the funds are low and the debts are high,
And you want to smile, but you have to sigh,
When care is pressing you down a bit,
Rest, if you must, but don't you quit.

Life is queer with its twists and turns,
As every one of us sometimes learns,
And many a failure turns about,
When he might have won had he stuck it out,
Don't give up though the pace seems slow –
You may succeed with another blow.

Often the goal is nearer than,
It seems to a faint and faltering man,
Often the struggler has given up,
When he might have captured the victor's cup,
And he learned too late when the night slipped down,
How close he was to the golden crown.

Success is failure turned inside out –
The silver tint of clouds of doubt,
And you never can tell how close you are,
It may be near when it seems so far,
So stick to the fight when you're hardest hit –
It's when things seem worst that you must not quit.

Love Handles: How many times have you grown weary of a situation and quit? How often have you held on until God changed your situation? Which was more beneficial to you, holding on or letting go?

Chapter 22

Let the Church Say A-MAN!

—∿∿—

Song of Solomon 5:16 — His mouth is sweetness itself; he is altogether lovely. This is my lover; this is my friend, O daughters of Jerusalem.

Countless times, I have run into young women who have grown tired of dealing with immature men. "Deliver me from little boys," one sister in Christ exclaimed as I ministered with her in the middle of a department store. I had not seen her in years but have known her since she was a little girl in elementary school. She had recently married, but during our conversation I learned that she was now divorced. "He was crazy, Eddie," she explained. "It was like a complete turn the day after we got married," she added. She went on to tell me of how his personal insecurities grew worse during the course of the marriage. He would accuse her of infidelity, speak negatively towards her in public, and even threaten her well being. She stated that she put up with it as long as she could and finally decided to bail out of the marriage. Of course, this was her side of the story without the benefit of hearing his point of view.

I hardly hear of the need for women to grow up and act their age; it is the man who is often on the receiving end of the question, "When are you going to grow up?" I Corinthians 13:11 states, *"When I was a child, I talked like a child; I thought like a child, I reasoned like a child. When I became a man, I put childish ways behind me."* I am convinced that the main reason men as a whole are not able to grasp the privileges of being Men of Destiny is because too many are spiritually immature. During my earlier days of immaturity, I recall hitting a low in my life. My college grade-point average dropped below standard. My friends were few, and my social life was the pits. Yet, all of this was because of my own doing not because of how others treated me; I was the immature one.

I remember driving west on Shelby Drive toward Lamar Avenue one afternoon with the radio off, talking to God about the lows I was experiencing in my life. Out of the clearness of His profound revelation, God allowed my eyes to focus on an outdoor advertisement that read, "Growing old is inevitable, but growing up is optional." Like a dagger, those words dug at the core of my issues and provided me insight regarding my breakthrough. I knew at this point that if I were ever going to rise above mediocrity, I had to make some changes in my life. I also realized that I had "shucked" my responsibility as a man of God. I was living irresponsibly and acting immaturely; I was out of control. In essence, I was trading God's blessing for me with what the world had to offer. But, at that very moment, the person I was in God's sight became real to me. You could say I had had an epiphany! The reality was that God had created me to be a leader and vessel for him.

In fact, men, we are unique creations! Unique, in that, we are privileged. After all, the Bible records that we were created first. In Genesis 2:7, when God formed man from the dust of the ground and breathed into his nostrils the breath of life, he gave man privilege. We have the privilege of giving life. If the naked truth were told, millions of sperm reside within a man's body waiting to ignite life. Thus, we (men) are privileged because we have been given authority and ordained to have dominion over habitation and home. On the contrary, several of us have compromised our destiny in God for a position in the enemy's camp. We have allowed our privilege as a man to be exchanged for some modern belief that we need to get in touch with our feminine side. No! God made male and female, not male-female or female-male. About the only thing more corrupt than a woman getting in touch with her masculinity is a man tapping into his "inner woman."

Bishop T.D. Jakes in his book <u>The Lady, Her Lover, and Her Lord</u> purports that many of us have abused the life within us by allowing it to fall into the wombs of women whose gardens we do not possess; in whose fields we have not owned, and in whose pastures we should not be grazing. In other words, because of drugs, gangs, incarceration, and neglect some men have voluntarily stepped aside in their households. Our women are left with the difficult task of teaching boys to be men. All the while, the truest examples and best teachers—men— are missing from the picture. Hence, a generation of boys is growing up without the benefit of seeing something as insignificant as a father shaving to something as critical as witnessing a father praying. Some of us remain in this perpetual state of boyhood while our younger males are slowly becoming endangered. In today's vernacular, I Corinthians 13:11 would read, "Back in the day when I was not only younger but also in the world, I played around too much. But, now that I've grown in my knowledge of Christ, I quit playing around and grew up."

Brothers in Christ, if I asked you the question, "When did you realize you had grown up and become a man?" many of you would likely answer as early as thirteen and some as late as forty. The numerous experiences encountered during the lifetime of a male leads him to manhood. For some it was moving out of their parent's home; yet for others it was fathering a child. However, so many others have not realized their manhood. Although in so many ways manhood is defined by the world's standards, the Word of God provides the best definition of manhood and the best examples of what it takes to become a man. If you want to know if a male is a man, then read I Corinthians 13:11. *"When I was a child, I spoke as a child, I understood as a child, I thought as a child, but when I became a man, I put away childish things."* This verse intimates that a man's language, longings, logic, and lifestyle serve as clues to his level of maturity. What determines a man? Use the following criteria to measure a man:

1st – Listen to his language.

Much like my son Trevor, babies do not have a good grasp of what to say, when to say it, or how to speak appropriately. Men, on the other hand, should have a firm grip of their tone and tongue.

In Proverbs 21:23, you find these words, "Whoever guards his mouth and tongue, keeps his soul from troubles." In other words, a man knows WHAT to say. Proverbs 25:11 says, "A word fitly spoken is like apples of gold in settings of silver." Therefore, a man should know WHEN to speak. Also, Proverbs 15:2 advises that, "The tongue of the wise uses knowledge rightly, but the mouth of fools pours forth foolishness." Lastly, a man should know HOW to speak appropriately.

Gone are the days for men to talk down to women or shout insults at those deemed to be weaker than they. To use words unbecoming of a Christian not only reveals much about a man's intelligence but also about his spiritual nature. In a nutshell, listen to a man's language and you will discover his level of maturity.

2nd – Analyze his thoughts and desires.
Consider a man's language and his longings. James 1:5-8 teaches that "a double minded man is unstable in all his ways." Men should not be confused about on which side of the fence to stand! Spiritually mature men "seek those things which are above and think on those things which are true, noble, just, pure, lovely, as well as those things which are of good report." (Philippians 4:8-9)

3rd – Recheck his reasoning or his logic.
In I Corinthians 14:20, Paul returns to those same folk found in chapter 13 and reminds the brothers to cease thinking and reasoning like children. Many of the problems we have in our homes, churches, or on our jobs could be avoided if we would stop and reason as mature people instead of like kids. Children say things that make sense to them whether they are right or wrong. You can not blame them because their reasoning is based on their limited life experiences.

Ladies, if you are dating a man who seems to talk in circles when the subject of a long-term commitment is brought up, then most likely he is not mature enough for a relationship with you. If it makes sense to him but baffles others, either your expectations are ill focused or he is not ready for the next level. Will he get there eventually? Maybe or maybe not! However, do not make the mistake of providing ultimatums. Ultimatums will not provide you the long-term commitment desired. When a man reasons that he is ready, then he must decide to make that move. Until then, you have to make a decision to ride his roller coaster of indecisions out for the long haul with no promise of ever arriving or walking away.

4th – Look at his lifestyle.
I Timothy 4:12 – Let no man despise thy youth; but be thou an example of the believers in word, in conversation, in

charity, in spirit, in faith, in purity. (KJV) That term "conversation" is interpreted "lifestyle." A man's lifestyle defines who he is, where he is going, and the company he keeps. Ladies, how does he spend his free time? Is he employed? Who are his best friends? What does he value? What does he despise?

Men, who are you when you are alone and no one is watching? Do you read and study the Word of God? Do you practice the teachings of your faith? Who are you, really? What are your goals? What type of company do you keep? Remember, mature Christian men should imitate the man described in Psalm 1 who "does not walk in the counsel of the wicked, nor stand in the path of sinners, nor sit in the seat of scoffers." In other words, you do not find this man hanging with *haters* or loafing with *losers*! But, mature men enjoy the Word of God and the people of God. It is in God's Word that you find him meditating day and night. As a result of this lifestyle of integrity, a mature man of God is like a tree that has been firmly planted by living water. And, every harvest season, you can spot him a mile away because of the fruit he yields. Everything he touches seems to prosper.

Meanwhile, the ultimate man shows up in the New Testament in the person of Jesus Christ. Let the church say A MAN! In I John 2:2, "He is the atoning sacrifice for our sins, and not only for ours but also for the sins of the whole world." What an awesome man God is! This is the only man whose actual blood makes a difference in our lives. This is the type of man we should all aspire to become, and indeed this is the type of man on whom women can depend.

It is one thing for a man's actions to affect us, but it is a whole other dynamic when his blood affects us greatly. The psalmist says about Jesus' blood that:

It soothes my doubts and calms my fears; and it dries all
my tears
It reaches to the highest mountain; it flows to the lowest
valley
The blood that gives me strength from day to day
It will never lose its power.

There are over forty references to the blood of Christ in the New Testament. The last reference, of course, appears in Revelation 12:11 – "They overcame him by the blood of the Lamb and by the word of their testimony." That is a powerful man whose blood causes us to overcome and be declared victorious. The blood of Christ is life-giving. The atoning blood of Jesus Christ has saved lives, renewed hopeless situations, and given life. I Peter 2:24 states, "He himself bore our sins in his body on the tree, so that we might die to sins and live for righteousness; by his wounds you have been healed."

Jesus bore the sins of the entire WORLD in his body while he hung on the cross at Calvary. Why is that significant? First, that means that He died for us all. It really should have been us paying the penalty for our sins, but Christ became our substitutionary atonement. He subbed for us when we could not do it for ourselves. This one redeeming act of selfless sacrifice is what reconciles us to God. Any amends have been made. Any reparation for injuries caused by our sins has been paid. In other words, his death removed our sin! What a man! When I did not even know myself, Christ died for me and literally died *as me* so that I would not have to suffer. Because he is as much man as he is God, he satisfied the requirement that God had in order to appease his wrath upon us. He made what was wrong completely right again which is why we are called righteous. It is not because I have done right, but because of what Christ has done for me that makes me righteous before a holy God.

Romans 5:8 – "But God demonstrates his own love for us in this: While we were still sinners, Christ died for us."

What an incredible Man! Knowing back then that I would be filthy and of no good use, Christ climbed up on a cross anyway and endured suffering for me. Romans 5:10 – "For if, when we were God's enemies, we were reconciled to him through the death of his Son, how much more, having been reconciled, shall we be saved through his life." Now, that is the kind of man we all should emulate.

Lastly, the blood of Jesus cleanses me from all filthiness. Truly **my confession of faith, my baptism, the preaching and teaching I offer, the praises I give, and even my giving and service are all in vain if the atoning factor of blood is removed.** In Leviticus 17:11 various types of offerings —burnt, sin, guilt, fellowship, and grain offering— had to be given for one to be cleansed. Hebrews 9:22b states, "... without the shedding of blood, there is no forgiveness." So, as gory as this may sound, He had to shed his blood in order for us to be saved. All of this being said, I have a responsibility to live for God and serve him wholeheartedly. Galatians 2:20 – "I have been crucified with Christ and I no longer live, but Christ lives in me. The life I live in the body, I live by faith in the Son of God, who loved me and gave himself for me." Because I have been crucified with Christ, I no longer live independently of Christ, but Christ lives in me!

If you have not experienced, acknowledged, and accepted the love of Christ and his salvation, then chances are you are walking in darkness. Allow the light that only comes from Him to illuminate your life and provide the direction and forgiveness that you long for in your life. Let the church say A-MAN!

Love Handles: Given your place in the ministry of God's kingdom in addition to considering your career/occupation, describe the qualities that your soul mate will need to possess to be a man.

Chapter 23

What's in Your Wallet?

—ɯ—

Romans 13:7-8 – *Give everyone what you owe him:*
If you owe taxes, pay taxes; if revenue, then revenue;
if respect, then respect; if honor, then honor. Let no
debt remain outstanding, expect the continuing debt
to love one another, for he who loves his fellowman
has fulfilled the law.

Capital One has initiated a series of commercials that
contains the catchy, inquiring phrase, "**What's In Your
Wallet**?" It is an important slogan for Singles to consider at
the inception of another year. We should check our wallets,
bank accounts, and budgets regularly in order to prevent a
mountain of debts from piling up. It would not hurt us to
revisit our monthly income to determine if our money is
working for or against us. The Word of God encourages us to
stay out of debt. Romans 13:8 states, "*Owe no one anything
except to love one another, for he who loves another has
fulfilled the law.*" (KJV) *The Living Bible* translates it as,
"Let no debt remain outstanding, except the continuing debt
to love one another, for he who loves his fellowman has
fulfilled the law."

In other words, love is the only debt that is never paid in full. It is, as the Reverend C.J. Finney puts it, the "one perpetual obligation." However, all other debts should be paid in full. While the Bible does not teach against borrowing per se, remaining in a position of outstanding debts is not God's desire for his people. Simply put, when we borrow, we are expected to pay back. When we purchase, we are expected to pay. When we hire help, we are expected to pay. Therefore, when creditors call for payment, we must pay up! It is the Christian thing to do. In fact, there is no need in getting upset or attempting to get even with the creditor by holding back the payment due them. A comment such as, "They'll get paid when I get paid," is not an appropriate or legitimate response to your creditors' right to seek payment. The key to your financial freedom is to *pay off* what you owe and to *pay it on time*.

According to the latest economic outlook, Americans are grossly in debt. In fact, Americans are loaded down with too many credit cards. As recently reported by Cardweb.com, the average American household has about $9,200 in credit debt. And, this amount is just for one credit card! The amount owed is exacerbated by the fact that most interest rates are in the teens (i.e. 13%-19%). Therefore, with most persons paying only the monthly minimum, it is no wonder staggering numbers of Singles remain grossly in debt. Because the major credit card companies recognize the deep pit many Americans are digging for themselves, in January 2006 they began doubling the minimum monthly payment that cardholders were required to pay. This was done in an effort to aid consumers in getting out of debt sooner. For the most part, the majority of our debt issues can be attributed to our lack of discipline and uncontrolled desire to catch up with the Jones', who I might add are also in debt.

The following are additional contributors to debt:

1. Desiring to purchase things that are not necessarily needed
2. Purchasing unaffordable items with a credit card
3. Coveting those things which are not within God's will
4. Doubting God's provision for our daily needs
5. Defaulting on credit card payments

Excessive or unchecked debt could damage our Christian testimony. To prevent injury to our walk of integrity, we must learn to reduce our debt and avoid the habit of ill-spending. The steps below provide a skeleton for such a transition:

Step 1 — Confess your mistakes in spending

No one can accept responsibility for mistakes in spending except you. Admit that you messed up and move on to Step 2.

Step 2 — Commit to a plan

Set your priorities and design a budget. I know it is a big word, but it works – BUDGET. In designing a budget, make certain you prioritize between the things you WANT versus the things you NEED. Additionally, cut back on the things you really do not need immediately. Control your spending. Plan to spend only a certain amount on food, leisure, and "I owe it to myself items." Make certain you do not borrow more than you can afford to pay back. Do not follow a plan for a month only to return to old habits the next month. Begin saving as little as $25 a month. Do not over save. Technically, you really cannot afford to save hugely with so much debt looming over your head. Believe it or not, this will yield $300 a year that can be continually added to or used to pay towards an outstanding debt.

Step 3 — Call your creditors and design a payment plan

I contacted my credit card companies and was actually able to negotiate a lower percentage rate. All you have to do is ask, in most cases; creditors are very competitive and will be willing to work deals to retain your account. Give it try, today.

Step 4 — Seek wise counsel

In other words, accept sound advice from financially savvy people. Often, they will inform you of places to find the best interest rates. Ask around your congregation and among business savvy individuals.

Step 5 — Give your tithes and offering to a growing ministry. Do not forget to give God a portion of the blessings he has bestowed upon you. It is one of the simplest ways out of debt. As contrary as it sounds, many have found themselves giving their way out of debt.

For more help in reducing your debt, you may benefit from reading Pat Robertson's booklet entitled *A Guide to Financial Freedom.* You may receive a free copy by calling **1-800-759-0700.** Another excellent resource is on line at **CNNMoney.com.** And remember, each of us has a debt greater than the monthly financial debt—the greatest debt owed. It is a SIN debt. But, it is only through Christ Jesus that we are forgiven of this debt. Accept Christ by faith as your personal savior and free yourself from the penalty of sin as well. You, too, can be debt free financially and spiritually!

Love Handles: Pray this prayer with me if you're serious about being free of debts. "Lord God almighty, I acknowledge you as the One true and living God. To you I owe my life. You are the giver of life and giver of all gifts. I come to your throne of grace asking for mercy. I am in debt and have made bad decisions regarding my finances. But, I know that you are able to deliver me from the vices of financial ruin. I turn my finances over to you and ask you to mold me into a worthy steward of what you have blessed me with in this life. To you be the glory!"

If you desire to be Spiritually saved from your sin debt, pray this prayer as well.

"God, I acknowledge you as supreme and your only begotten son, Jesus Christ, as Saviour of this world. I have sinned and fallen short of your word. I am sorry for my actions. But, because I know that your son died for my sins, I ask forgiveness through his blood. Today, I ask that you renew me and impart the gift of the Holy Spirit in me. I invite you into my life and accept the gift of salvation through your son Christ Jesus. I love you and today begin serving you with my whole heart, mind, and soul. AMEN.

Chapter 24

A Good Thing is NOT Hard to Find

—⧖—

Proverbs 18:22 — *He who finds a wife, finds what is good and receives favor from the LORD.*

Where does a single man begin his search of this good thing—a wife? To fully understand the task before him, it is imperative that the Word of God be used as his spiritual navigational system. In a sermon entitled *How to Find a Godly Wife*, Robert Deffinbaugh outlines five steps that every single man should follow when seeking a wife. That same week I received his sermonic notes, ironically, I had been studying Genesis 24: 1-67. I noticed a strong parallel between the story of Abraham's search for Isaac's wife and the five points that Deffinbaugh exposes in his sermon on finding a godly wife. Let us explore...

The story that follows in Genesis 24 is a beautiful account of how God's divine intervention works to bring his ultimate plan into fruition. The imagery and ideals portrayed in this passage of scripture are simply masterful. The story begins with the picture of an elderly, blessed Abraham who the Bible records was not only old but also "well stricken in age." But, within that same passage, we find that he was also "blessed in all things." Oh, if we all could see that despite our age, God has truly blessed us in all things as well. Sure, we feel that we could use more of everything we have already, but if God does not add to what He has given to us, He has already been more than generous.

Yet, this passage is not about Abraham. Instead, it is about his son Isaac's future. Abraham makes his eldest servant vow that he would not choose a wife for his son from among the Canaanites but from Abraham's former country. Even if Eliezar was able to locate Isaac a wife, he feared because of the distance required to travel back that the woman may refuse the offer. Abraham assured Eliezar that if the woman chosen should refuse to travel the distance, Eliezar would be free from the oath the two had made. Therefore, Eliezar packs up and gathers ten more servants as they adventure to Mesopotamia. There they stop at a watering hole. It is here that Eliezar prays that God reveal Isaac's wife to him by allowing the woman God had chosen to offer not only to provide water to him and his group of servants but also to Eliezar's camels. What? The camels too. Well, just as soon as he finished that prayer, Rebecca approaches the watering hole and personifies all for which Eliezar had just prayed. She offered not only Eliezar water but his camels as well. What a mighty God we serve! Talk about being in the right place at the appointed time. Wow!

Later, Eliezar meets Rebecca's parents and explains his reason for coming. After much discussion, Rebecca agrees to travel back with Eliezar to meet Isaac. When they return to Canaan, she spots Isaac from afar and inquires about who he is. Covering herself and dismounting her camel, she and Isaac walk toward one another. I guess you can call it love at first sight because immediately the two of them entered his mother's tent and consummated their union. Within this text, lie some critical points for single men in search of a wife and a refreshing view of the actions of a single woman being pursued. Examine these crucial points for yourself.

POINT 1: Paraphrasing Deffinbaugh's take on this passage of scripture, *when a man is in search of a wife, he must first take personal inventory.* In other words, a man must seek a wife *only* when he is certain that the institution of marriage will achieve the purpose that God has for both his life as well as that of his wife's. Isaac's wife would later play a vital role in helping him carry out the plan God had for his life. It would be Isaac who would continue what God had begun in Abraham. Therefore, it was crucial that he chose the "right" helpmate to be by his side. As long as they both walked in agreement, they would both benefit from what God would ultimately do in their lives. Likewise, single men of destiny should understand the effect of having an ordained wife versus just another female by their side. The right person next to you can mean the difference between success and failure. My wife was ordained for me to realize the fullness of what God has for me. Just another female in my corner would have threatened, sabotaged, or even aborted the mission God has planned for me.

Brothers, understand that God has invested too much in you to lead you to a woman whose destiny is not in line with yours. Some of us have been criticized for being too selective. So what! When it comes to carrying out the promises of God, there is no such thing as being too prudent or even too selective. In fact, when you value what God has invested in you, it is counterproductive to allow the wrong person to enter your life. Moreover, if the person you choose is not going in the same direction or does not compliment your walk in Christ, then chances are she is not *the one!* You have permission to move on.

One final note on this point needs to be stressed. People will often create all sorts of agendas for you if you allow them. Therefore, check out what God has to say about your marital state. He may have blessed you with the gift of singleness; therefore, looking for a mate is futile. Or, His will for your life may be that you share your life with your soul mate – the one lover specifically crafted for you. If the latter be the case, then let us go on to point #2.

POINT 2: *A man in search of a wife should <u>wait for God's timing</u>*. Ecclesiastes 3:1 states, "To everything, there is a season or a time to every purpose under the heaven." Everything that God does is according to his time schedule. I am sorry if you think that every person thirty-plus years old should be married by now. God's clock has a different movement. In my earlier years being confused about God's timing for a wife for me, an elder in the church stated to me, "Baby, you do know that there is something worse than not being married at all. Worse than not being married is being married to the wrong person." I will always cherish those words because in God's own time, He allows a harvest to occur in our lives—if we just wait on Him. Isaac was not ready for Rebekah until God sounded the wake up call. Likewise, Rebekah had to be certain that God was orchestrating the events of her life.

It took a while to travel from Abraham's place to Rebekah's home and back, especially via the camel express. She had plenty of time to process her expectations and to determine if this was truly within God's will. I can imagine the anticipation Rebekah must have experienced during the entire journey—"Is he going to be cute? What are his interests? Will I be what he finds pleasure in for a lifetime? Does he love God with his whole mind, heart, and soul?" And, certainly, Isaac must have experienced similar thoughts—"I hope she is fine…Lord I hope she is not ugly!" No, seriously. He likely wondered, "Is she going to be a good mother to my children? Will her attitude be pleasant? Will she respect me at all times? Will my family adore her as much as I cherish her?" Only time would provide the answers to these mysteries.

Brothers, on the one hand, she may be *right* for you but at this time she may not be *ripe* for you! As much as I love mangos, I must admit, the ones that are ripe have a sweetness that cannot be compared to any other fruit. But, ripeness takes time. Likewise, personalities, visions, purposes, goals, and even spiritual growth all take time to ripen. Therefore, to move in front or ahead of God is to commit spiritual suicide. In addition, acting prematurely is akin to removing fruit from a vine before it has had time to fully sweeten. So, slow down, take time and *wait* on God to develop you and your mate for such a time that you both can enjoy the sweetness of one another.

Point 3: *A man in search of a wife should look in the right places and be in his righteous mind.* Abraham decided to broaden his circle of choices and not limit his search. He instructed his servant Eliezar to return to his former country to find Isaac's wife. The local women were Canaanites and were known for their sexual sins. This type of woman would not have been a good fit for the promises God had in mind for Isaac and his off springs. This idea has an even deeper meaning for those brothers who are seeking mates without regard for cultural, spiritual, or even moral connectivity. Some of us have been looking in all the wrong places. And, the sad fact is that we find ourselves revisiting the same wrong places in hopes of finding the right person—only to come up empty every time! Please know that the key to a successful search begins with prayer. The servant in Genesis 24:12 prayed for God's direction and God revealed his answer—Rebekah.

When it comes to his thoughts, a single man cannot afford to be narrow-minded. Just as narrow roads make for dangerous passages, narrow thinking leads to distorted views. For so many, the pursuit of marriage is more about narrow thinking—sexuality and personality. To view marriage as an opportunity for legal sex is a total distortion of God's intended purpose. Consequently, those who limit their scope to such inconsistencies are in for a rude awakening the morning after the honeymoon. Rather, under a broader scope marriage should be seen as an opportunity for ministry and shared, unconditional love (with several benefits including uninhibited, unashamed sexual pleasure among them all).

In Genesis 24:27, Eliezar states, "...I being in the way, the Lord led me to the house of my master's brethren." He did not mean that he was an obstacle or hindrance to God by being *in the way*. Rather, he was indicating his will and purpose was *in line with* or *going in the same direction as* God's will and purpose. In short, he was in a righteous frame of mind while seeking a wife for Isaac. And therefore, he looked in the right places for her.

Step 4: *Godly men in search of wives must seek godly qualities in a woman.* In Eliezar's prayer, he asked God specifically for an order of events to occur. He asked that the woman for Isaac not only provide water for him to drink but for his camels to drink as well. Now, on the surface it does not seem like much of a request, but a closer look reveals some godly qualities that are valuable when searching for a helpmate. This one act of kindness speaks volumes. I see gentleness, goodness, faith, meekness, temperance, humbleness, and self-control. You got it — the fruits of the Holy Spirit (Galatians 5:22-23). To care for my needs is a blessing; however, to provide for my camels is truly amazing.

Brothers, what are the camels in your home? For some of us, it may be our ministry. A correctly chosen wife is willing to offer relief or to help you meet the demands of your ministry which is *your camel*. Still for others, your camel may be an extended family member or a child from a previous relationship. Nevertheless, whatever your camels are, know that their care is your primary responsibility. Yet, there is considerable comfort and peace of mind in knowing that you have someone together with you who is willing to share the weight and assist you in attending to their needs. Though Rebekah's beauty possibly faded with time, her godly qualities of gentleness and love proved more beneficial to the continued life of her marriage to Isaac.

Step 5: *Finally, a man in search of a wife should be willing to heed the counsel of older and wiser Christians.* When Eliezar swore to carry out Abraham's command, he placed himself in line with God's will. God is so awesome in the way he arranges circumstances perfectly for His will to be fulfilled. Whenever we find ourselves walking in obedience, God will show Himself faithful every time. God led the servant to the **right** place at the **right** time to meet the **right** woman. Glory to God!

Singles, the counsel of older and wiser saints is paramount in your quest for a wife. Let us now examine the direction given in scripture:

Proverbs 4:7— Wisdom is the principal thing: therefore, get wisdom: and with all thy getting, get understanding. (KJV)

Proverbs 11:14— Where no counsel is, the people fall: but in the multitude of counselors, there is safety. (KJV)

Proverbs 16:16— How much better is it to get wisdom than gold...

Proverbs 19:20— Listen to advice and accept instruction, and in the end you will be wise.

Indeed, every man should have someone in his life (a father, an uncle, grandfather, coach, pastor, mother, grandmother, and so on) that exemplifies wisdom and godliness. These are the persons to whom we must go in the hour of our search for a wife. Not only can wise individuals guide our selections but also they can confirm our choices. Be blessed in your search for a good thing!

Love Handles: How is this chapter speaking to you personally?

Chapter 25

I liked It Better
When I Was Single

—⟋𝔪⟍—

I Corinthians 7:26-28 — *Because of the present crisis, I think that it is good for you to remain as you are. Are you married? Do not seek a divorce. Are you unmarried? Do not look for a wife. But if you do marry, you have not sinned; and if a virgin marries, she has not sinned. But, those who marry will face many troubles in this life, and I want to spare you this.*

Imagine the shock I displayed upon hearing from a married friend that he was not enjoying his marriage at all. "Man, Eddie, I liked it better when I was single," he said in disgust.

"What!" I shouted. "What do you mean that you liked it better when you were single?"

I could hardly believe what I was hearing. This was coming from the mouth of someone I considered happily married. From the outward appearance, it seemed he had the happiest life with his family; they were a couple with a lot of promise for the future. However, his lips revealed more of the actuality of his marriage. Beneath the surface festered a boiling pot of jealously, resentment, verbal abuse, financial woes, and spiritual warfare. But, what marriage has not been asked to survive under non-perfect terms, I thought to myself. I mean, should all married couples question the possibility that two imperfect individuals could unite under the guidance of a perfect God?

"I liked it better when I was single," kept ringing in my ears the days before I said, "I do." Sure, it bothered me, but it did not make me question what I was embarking upon. Instead, his statement haunted me because I wanted to know what goes wrong in relationships such as this and how I could help reconcile the differences of other couples in this same situation. This gave me pause, and I remembered the words of William Somerset Maugham who said, "We are not the same persons this year as last; nor are those we love. It is a happy chance if we, changing, continue to love a changed person." In other words, people change! So, it is really a miracle of love if we can still remain married to the ever-changing person we call a spouse.

I guess that is why the Apostle Paul was quick to warn the Singles at Corinth of the dynamics surrounding marriage. He warned them that should they decide to marry their lives would present a whole other set of challenges and problems. They are the type of problems best handled with two people touching and agreeing. It was then that I realized this was the first thing missing from my friend's marriage. He and his wife were not touching and agreeing on anything nor were they praying or even worshiping together. Even during their courtship, they did not pray together. Thereby, it was inevitable that their marriage would not be one guided by prayer either.

Shortly after this conversation with my friend, I attended the wedding of one of our mutual friends. Hoping to get a different view of marriage during this ceremony, I sadly left more despondent than ever before. The bride was not happy and questioned her relationship with the groom. It was not until I picked up the Word of God and read about a wedding at Cana that I learned more about marriage than I had ever anticipated. It was the word of God that gave me back my hope for a promising future as a husband.

In John 2:1-11, the passage reads "On the third day a wedding took place at Cana in Galilee. Jesus' mother was there, and *Jesus and his disciples had also been invited* to the wedding. When the wine was gone, Jesus' mother said to him, "They have no more wine." "Dear woman, why do you involve me?" Jesus replied, "My time has not yet come." His mother said to the servants, "Do whatever he tells you." Nearby stood six stone water jars, the kind used by the Jews for ceremonial washing, each held from twenty to thirty gallons. Jesus said to the servants, "Fill the jars with water"; so they filled them to the brim. Then he told them, "Now draw some out and take it to the master of the banquet." They did as requested and the master of the banquet tasted the water that had been turned into wine. He did not realize from where it had come, though the servants who had drawn the water knew. After that he called the bridegroom aside and said, "Everyone brings out the choice wine first and then the cheaper wine after the guests have had too much to drink; but you have saved the best till now." This, the first of his miraculous signs, Jesus performed in Cana of Galilee. He thus revealed his glory, and his disciples put their faith in him.

Aha! The keys to a successful marriage were right before my eyes. This is where my friends had gone wrong. It was in the early stages of their single dating to the latter stages of their marriage that several key factors should have occurred. Referencing the scriptures, it is apparent that the first and most crucial piece that needs to take place is the *extension of an invitation* to accept Jesus Christ as Saviour. The very first two verses let us know that Jesus was an invited guest at the wedding in Cana. Therefore, it is important that God be invited into the relationship from the very beginning. His presence makes a difference.

Secondly, we discover the benefits of having *the Almighty's presence* in any marriage or relationship. When the couple ran out of wine and had exhausted their supply, they had to listen to the Savior. With Christ as the wise head of a marriage or a relationship, he becomes the advisor for all troubling situations. Running out of wine is tantamount to running out of money, running low of patience, or running dry of love. Instead of turning to friends or the world for a solution, they *listened* to Jesus. And, it was Jesus who was able to replenish what was depleted. In verse 8, he draws from the very vessel that they thought was depleted. Ironically, the fresh batch that Jesus touched was apparently sweeter than the batches before.

Looking at the latter part of the passage, there is one last factor that was present. The couple maintained a guest list with *partners of accountability*. They surrounded themselves with people who wanted to see them succeed. Their guest list was not filled with individuals they wanted to impress; rather, their list was made up of people who had left an impression on them. Even in the dating stage, you must be careful about whom you invite into your relationship. Believe it or not, there are people who desire to see relationships fail because their relationships were never successful. Individuals with unsuccessful relationships waste no time tearing others' apart which is the reason that my wife and I are careful and even intentional about whom we invite into our relationship. Moreover, to maintain the integrity of our marriage, we do not invite anyone to our home. And, even the circle of friends and family we keep are understood to be those who genuinely want to see us succeed as a family.

In a newspaper advice column, a wife wrote that her husband had grown lazy and that her love and passion for him had grown cold. She was now having thoughts of reuniting with her ex-boyfriend from years past. In fact, she now found herself longing to have a relationship with her former lover. The columnist responded to the wife, "You need to work on your marriage and forget rekindling an old flame that obviously died out years ago for a good reason." This was sage advice that I eventually passed on to my friend for him to work on his marriage. He had the responsibility of making it what he wanted it to be. And, if he truly loved his wife and was committed to the vows he had made before God, then he would get to work quickly. I informed him, as I remind myself from time to time that you have to work on the problems that surface in your marriage. Even if the two of you are not working together, at least one of you must be at the helm of the ship steering. If no one is steering then you will run aground and become shipwrecked.

I like to think of it in terms of a leaky ceiling in a million dollar mansion; or as a five carat diamond ring with a slightly visible flaw; or a 2009 Mercedes Benz with a flat tire. All of these things are fixable and worth keeping. I would not abandon a mansion with a leaky ceiling that could be repaired. And, I definitely would not trade in a 2009 luxury automobile because of a flat tire. Nor do I know of too many people who would toss a diamond ring aside because of a flaw. Replacing it with another would not work either because the nature of the diamond guarantees there will be flaws. Consequently, realize that anything worth having is worth fixing!

Love Handles: Do you have married friends who are unhappy with their marriages and regret their decisions to marry? If so, how can you encourage them to hold true to the vows they have taken?

Chapter 26

Bachelor Party Alternative

—ᴍ—

Ephesians 4:29 — *Do not let any unwholesome talk come out of your mouths, but only what is helpful for building others up according to their needs, that it may benefit those who listen.*

Very few men openly share with the world what occurred on the night of their Bachelor's Party. But, what I experienced does not equate to the stories I have heard from other married men. And, quite frankly, it does not even compare to bachelor parties I have attended in the past. With the ministers of my local church conspiring with my little brother and other long time best friends from high school and college, I did not know what to expect for my last night as a bachelor. I only knew that each of these men knew my walk, and I trusted that they would not jeopardize my testimony. Given that their walk was one of integrity, I had to trust that these men of God would not exchange one night of simple pleasures for a lifetime of guilt and shame. But, you can never know for sure!

My best friend from high school, Trennie, and my brother Mario arrived at my home early in the evening. Their task was to escort me to an undisclosed location and ensure my safe arrival. They were both very secretive about the agenda for that night and seemed quite enthused and eager to get started. When I inquired about plans for the evening, they just remarked, "You're not in charge tonight, Bud! Just ride and enjoy yourself. We've got this!" For me, this was scary! As we rode, I prayed. "Lord, please keep my attitude right and please don't let these boys plan something stupid." At this juncture, I was on the verge of beginning a life with someone I had waited an entire lifetime to meet. I did not need the beginning of my marriage to start off rocky because of some stupid actions such as drinking, stripping, or wild sex. Therefore, you can imagine my surprise when my friend pulled onto the parking lot of a local strip club.

As he parked the car, I sat motionless, pondering whether to go along with what these guys had planned and run the risk of shaming God and my future wife or to protest, remain in the car, stand my ground, and refuse to compromise my standards. I had come too far in my growth in Christ to trade it in on peer pressure. I was thirty-nine years old and to me, this was high school mess! The more I protested, the more insistent the guys became. In fact, they were already on the phone talking to the rest of the ministers and friends who were reportedly inside the club awaiting my arrival. I stepped out of the truck reluctantly, protesting all the way to the front door. As I looked up, I realized that I was compromising; I remained frozen in my steps. My friend offered to pay my way, but I continued to stand paralyzed. The look upon my face must have been enough for them to let me off the hook. I had been tricked! The rest of the guys were NOT inside the club. Rather, they all were waiting at a restaurant downtown. The entire act had been staged.

Of course, by this time, everyone including the bouncer was in stitches laughing at my disbelief. "We got him good guys," my friend remarked as he detailed what had just happened to the others who had been assembled downtown.

Upon our arrival downtown, we were told that our wait time would be a while. This was perhaps one of the most pivotal points of the night. As we sat by a piano in the lobby, the brothers began to tell me of their admiration for me and of how much they valued the relationships I had with them. And, at this point, one by one, they began to pour out words of encouragement and inspiration into my spirit. One at a time, bits of advice and counsel streamed into my consciousness. Even after we were seated, the conversation deepened. Daryl chimed in, "Brother, is there anything you would like to ask of the men sitting around the table?" Understand that when you wait to get married as long as I did, your friends are likely either all married or have experience marriage and divorce. So, basically, wisdom and experience were at my disposal. Proverbs 27:17 states, "As iron sharpens iron, so one man sharpens another." These brothers were literally about to sharpen a new piece of iron.

I asked each of them intimate questions such as:

1. What, if anything, did they regret about being married?
2. What would they change if they could?
3. What, in their opinion, keeps the marriage going?
4. What sexual tips for keeping a wife satisfied were they willing to share?

Now, that last question came as you recall from earlier chapters as a result of over twelve years of abstinence. It had been since my late twenties when I was last in a sexual relationship. This was by choice that I cut myself completely off from sexual encounters and exercise restraint and self-discipline until marriage. As active as I had become, I never knew what it meant to truly make love to a woman. But, when it came to the lust factor, I had that perfected and mastered. So, being able to make love for the first time in life was bound to be scary and exciting at the same time!

Throughout the wee hours of the night, the conversation about life, happiness, spiritual growth, and women grew more intense. It was a night to remember and cherish. And, it was an evening that actually gave pep to my step into matrimony. Because of this candid advise, I went into the marriage with loads of confidence and affirmed trust that God would not let me fail at the covenant He was about to establish.

Would you like to know what their advice to me was? Well, I am delighted you asked.

Regarding question #1 – What, if anything, did they regret about being married? None of the men shared regrets but a few did note that they were disappointed with the reality of marriage. They commented that they had constructed this image of about what marriage was going to be. When it did not quite measure up to their expectations, they were more disappointed than regretful.

Regarding question #2 — What would they change about their marriage that would make it better from the beginning? This one was unanimous. They advised me to keep other people out of our business from the very beginning. This included friends, co-workers, and family members. "Keep the affairs of your marriage as tightly confident as the security at Ft. Knox," one brother emphatically advised.

Regarding question #3 — What, in their opinion, keeps a marriage going? The fellows commented, "Jones, keep your wife your first priority." They added, if I treat my wife like a queen, that in return I would be regarded as a king. "Family comes first," they all agreed. Other advisements included keeping the relationship fresh and exciting and not predictable; communicating openly and honestly about EVERYTHING; and purposely protecting the integrity of the marriage even if it means detaching yourself from unhealthy friendships and family members.

Regarding question #4 — What sexual tips for keeping my wife satisfied were they willing to share? The room lit up with excitement and one by one each began to chime in with responses to this question. I will share the PG-13 version of their advice. "Satisfy her first!" One brother noted, "You can always get yours!" As if that was not plain and clear enough, another friend added, "Don't think of it as a chore, but learn to enjoy each other. You belong to her and she belongs to no one else but You!" The wisdom of the group shared, "Listen to her body and follow where she's taking you. I'm still listening to my wife after years of marriage."

The guys assured me that if I followed this advice and sprinkled my wife with lots of love, my marriage would last forever. It has been over a year now, and it seems they were right!

Love Handles: Below, please describe your ideal Bachelor or Bachelorette Bash! Who would be there? What activities would occur? Where would it take place? What would be the agenda for the event?

Closing Thoughts

—ɷ—

Appreciating Your Life

—⁓—

Psalm 139:14 – *I praise you because I am fearfully and wonderfully made; your works are wonderful, I know that full well.*

B ecause you are God's craftsmanship, you are special and not JUNK. Singles, God does not make junk! Despite how you feel about yourself on days when you have sinned and fallen short of God's mercy, you are fearfully and wonderfully made. Do not devalue your life but learn to appreciate your life. There are at least six ways to appreciate your life:

• **Remember that your life is Precious.**
　(Psalm 72:14) "He will rescue them from oppression and violence, for precious is their blood in his sight." Anything precious should be treated with care and concern. A precious piece of jewelry is handled differently from a piece of junk. Consequently, do not allow others to treat you less than what you are valued. Your life is near and dear to God and you. When a little girl is fretful over the loss of her favorite doll, this indicates to me that the girl regards her doll as more than just a toy. To her, the doll is *precious*. The cuff links given to me by my parents are not the most expensive pair I own, but they are the most *precious*. Each gold link contains a

silver embedded dime with their birth year inscribed. And, because they are *precious* to me, I only wear them on very special occasions. Your life should be treated in the same manner. To lose it would be devastating and to wear it casually as if it has no meaning would prove disastrous. Your life is *precious*.

- **Remember that your life is Priceless.**

(Matthew 10:31) "...you are worth more than many sparrows." In fact, if you look at verse 30, it is evident that we are *priceless* because even the hairs on our head are numbered. Now, that is priceless! For this reason, no one except God can put a price tag of worth on you. Anything less than what God declares you to be is inaccurate. The price of the body parts for a human being would perhaps barely add up to a thousand dollars. However, the price of a human life cannot be measured in dollar amounts; you are expensive in God's sight. He has invested gifts in you that no billionaire would be able to afford. The time he took crafting you and me into living souls alone is worth more than all of the world's jewelry. *You are priceless.* Even the enemy knows your value. That is why our souls are so valuable to him. Your life is priceless.

- **Remember that your life is Unique.**

(Genesis 1:27) "So God created man in his own image; in the image of God he created him; male and female He created them." (KJV) We are created in the very image of God; we are a reflection of God. That makes us *unique* - more unique than the stars, animals, mountains, or trees. Even our relationship with God is unique. Jeremiah 1:5 states, "Before I formed thee in the belly, I knew thee; and before thou camest forth out of the womb, I sanctified thee, and I ordained thee a prophet unto the nations." KJV *You are unique*! Like a snowflake or a human fingerprint, there is none like you. Your physical, mental, and emotional make-up cannot be compared to anyone else. The combination does not exist because you are unique. Celebrate the fact that you are unique; cease to be like everyone else. Surprisingly, they may be trying to be just like you. Recognize that you are *unique*!

• **Remember that you are God's chosen and He loves you.**
(Matthew 22:14) "Many are called but few are chosen." (KJV) Everyone has *not* been selected for service. Peter 2:9 states, "But, you are a chosen people, a royal priesthood, a holy nation, a people belonging to God, that you may declare the praises of him who called you out of darkness into his wonderful light." (KJV) God loves you and allows his face to shine upon you every morning. You have been chosen to serve and display the love of God to mankind. Walk with the assurance that your life is selected to give him Glory! Everything you do, say, and think should glorify our Heavenly Father.

• **Remember that you can think for yourself.**
(Romans 12:1-2) "Therefore, I urge you, brothers, in view of God's mercy, to offer your bodies as living sacrifices, holy and pleasing to God – this is your spiritual act of worship. Do not conform any longer to the pattern of this world, but be transformed by the renewing of your mind. Then you will be able to test and approve what God's will is – his good, pleasing and perfect will." This year, think for yourself and stop allowing others to influence your decision. They do not have to live with the consequences of your wrong decisions, nor should they be allowed to claim the glory that comes from good decisions. You are accountable to your own body and life. So, think wisely and use sound judgment.

• **Believe that you can say "No" without feeling guilty.**

(James 4:7) "Submit yourselves, then, to God. Resist the devil, and he will flee from you." When people come to you with disorder such as gossip, greed, or games, tell them, "No, thanks" without feeling guilty. Say NO to mess from this point forward in your life! Say NO to others' agendas for your life especially those that do not fit into God's plan for you. Say NO to abusive treatment, foul language, and anything that brings harm to your mind, body, and soul. And, at the end of the day, refuse to feel guilty about it!

Recite this weekly: My life is *precious, priceless, and unique*. Therefore, I must be chosen by God and loved by God. This week, I can think for myself and say no without feeling guilty.

What They Did Not Preach On Sunday Morning

—ᴡᴠ—

Genesis 6:11-12 – Now the earth was corrupt in God's sight and was full of violence. God saw how corrupt the earth had become, for all the people on earth had corrupted their ways.

Within one year, two young members of our congregation were dead. One was killed by her husband and the other by her former boyfriend. During that same year, it seemed as if every other night, news reports were aired about local female victims of sexual violence. That following year, as we organized our first Singles' Conference, I knew that sexual violence needed to be one of the sessions offered. Sexual violence can take on many forms that include sexual harassment, intimidation, unsolicited touching, and even rape. In any of these forms, the problem is grave in this country. The Center for Disease Control (CDC) reported in 2007 that four percent of high school males and eleven percent of high school females were forced to have sex. Nearly one fourth of college women reported being the victim of an attempted or completed rape. Altogether, one in six women and one in thirty-three men noted that they had experienced sexual violence during their lifetime.

Of course, a number of these incidents go unreported because of the victim's fear that the law cannot assist them or the embarrassment they feel. Many victims are repeatedly attacked and silenced by physical coercion and by the threat of possible harm to family members if reported. Victims suffer the mental strain of such attacks and run the risk of developing long term health problems including sexually transmitted diseases. According to the CDC, in 2007, 32,000 pregnancies were the result of rapes. Most often, rapes are committed by intimate partners or family members. From date rape to domestic violence, I want you to be informed as to where to seek help.

Places of Assistance

- **Men Can Stop Rape** - An organization that targets young men, encouraging them to take action to prevent violence against women (www.mencanstoprape.org)
- **Rape, Abuse, and Incest National Network Hotline** (800-656-HOPE)
- **Violence Against Women Network** (www.vawnet. org)
- **STOP IT NOW!** (www.stopitnow.org)

A Letter From God

To Singles:

If I wanted to bring you into a wealthy place and position in your life at this very moment, could I trust you with prosperity?

If I clapped my hands of favor upon your household and spread my anointing upon you, could I entrust that power in your hands?

To the single parent, I need to know that I can entrust my angel—your child—into your hands. How you treat him or her is a direct indictment on the love that you have for me. You must nurture them as I have nurtured you.

Singles, if I allowed your path to intersect with the footsteps of your Soul-mate, could I trust you with my daughter or my son?

Single Ministers, can I trust you with the ministry that I have placed in your spirit? The ministry I have birthed in you is precious and worth protecting. Its value is determined by what you put into it.

I believe in you and love you…

Your heavenly father,
God

To Contact the Author
Visit his website: **www.emarceljones.com**

Printed in the United States
136874LV00002B/178/P

9 781607 911357